First Date Next Mate

Perspectives in Dating the "Next" Time Around

Elizabeth B. Lewis

ISBN: 978-1-5356-0097-2

In loving memory of Wes Lewis.
If you were still here, this book would not have been
written.

Dedicated to all my single friends looking for love. Hoping all will support each other's path while looking for love.

Contents

Introduction

THE ORIGINAL TITLE OF THIS book was going to be called *Dating 911*. That title had two meanings: my husband died on 9/11/05 when my kids were 9 and 11 and I wouldn't be in the dating world if I hadn't become a widow. Also, 911 is the number we call in case of emergency. Even though dating does not often entail dire "emergencies," there *are* times we wish we knew what to do or say right then and there! That's where this book will come in handy as a good resource.

You know that time when you get that text after a first meet or someone asks you out and you really don't want to go? What do you say? How do you give the kind no and not lead him/her on? Should you give the silent no and hope s/he gets the picture? Some are not sure how to flirt. You don't always know what to say when someone attractive approaches you. Or what if you are interested in someone? Even the most confident men/women don't know what to say. Lying comes back to bite you and many times you have to lie again to cover lie number one. So don't lie. You can say no *and* be kind about it. It is what it is, right? You can't manufacture love or adoring feelings. They're either there or they're not. When dating, you have to develop a thick skin and *not* take it personally.

There are many, many good people in the world (you're one of them) who are just not a good match for whatever reason. It doesn't make either of you bad. *But* be kind. Always! How do you know that his/her best friend won't end up being your Mr./Mrs. Right? The fact that you're reading this book should tell you that you're open to learning and you're "working" on yourself to become a better version of you! Both men and women like others that "work" on themselves to become better. So good for you! You rock!

Over the years that I've been in the dating world (I have dated since 2008) I've learned a lot, made some mistakes (okay, maybe more mistakes than I'd like to admit publically) and have talked through many a dating scenario. (My dating consulting clients get full access to me between sessions so I answer many texts and emails in between sessions). I'm a retired teacher and now a Life Coach/Dating Consultant; I simply help singles date. I'm not a "Hitch" or a matchmaker; I'm not an expert. I'm a coach. A coach who has played the dating game, understands it and wants to help others successfully navigate through it. I help singles identify and honor their values; I help them look at different perspectives in dating; and I help them pick one that works best for them. Then, as soon as you have it figured out, guess what? You change your mind! That's okay! You change your mind (not your values) as you go along because you are learning. You "learn to discern" to make better decisions with each new experience. You change with what you want. What you like.

What you don't like. In the end, the goal is arriving at a better YOU made with confidence and positivity.

I'd like this book to be practical, useful, and maybe give you perspectives you've not thought about in the past. Remember the word *perspective*. That is a big part of this. I may not even agree with some of the perspectives I present here, but I've learned about these different ways of thinking as I've muddled my way through dating and I'd like to share as much as I can with you. There's no way to cover it all because every situation is unique, but I'll hit the highlights. Take away the parts that resonate with you, skip over (or come back later to) the rest. Thoughts/thinking usually change very quickly in the dating world. But, just remain open to hearing different ways of thinking. Some of these things can only be grasped by going through the process and then reflecting. Reflection is *key*! Throughout this book, I'll give you Reflection Questions about which to ponder.

My writing *will* have a Christian viewpoint, but I'm also a realist and know everyone does not think like I (luckily that's what makes the world a more interesting place). I am more aware now what truly goes on in the dating world the "next" time around. I was/am shocked by some things I've learned. You might be, too. My married friends who read this might *really* freak out at some of this information! (Stay married!) I'll candidly talk about what I've learned, experienced and observed.

Dating the second time around (or third or fourth) is much different than when we were young in our 20's. That's why I've changed the title to *First Date, Next Mate*. Hopefully the information in this book will get you from your first date to your next mate. Many have told me over the years that I should write a book. I never thought I had any different information than the other dating books out there. There are many good books written by great experts and therapists/psychologists. I agree with so much that's been written. I'll quote some of those people and books/perspectives and share with you what I have learned from those books. I have a weekly dating support group I host in my home, where we talk about the many issues in dating. I give summaries of good books. We watch videos and talk about different dating perspectives.

What I decided to do with this book is combine all that I've learned (from the many books I've read, videos I've watched, listening in my dating support group, sermons heard, blogs read, my own dating life, my girlfriends, my guy friends, being enmeshed with singles, my radio show guests, etc.). I put all the most valuable learnings in one book as a reference to those who have found themselves in the single's world again. This book will be best for the divorced/widowed/the second or more time around that are marriage-minded, but will also be useful for those younger who have not found love after college and/or never married. If you don't ever want to remarry, that's okay. Again, take the parts that are useful and discard the rest.

One thing to remember before we begin: it *is* possible to love more than one person in a lifetime. There are many potential partners with whom you could be happy. The human heart has a great capacity to love. Our heads get fixed on "The One," as if there is only one person we can ever love. We compare this "one" to the fantasy we have in our minds. Usually this is a manufactured idea of what he or she will look and be like. We just won't love the same way as we did our deceased or ex-spouse. A common question in the single's world is, "Where are all the good men or women?" My answer is, God gives them to us every day. It's up to us to decide if they are right for us. It's not God's "fault" that you're not in relationship or in the wrong relationship. It's the "free will" God allowed that enables us to decide. Fortunately, God gives us intuition to figure out if/why someone isn't good for us. Our gut (which I call the Holy Spirit) often knows the answer. It is important to look at each person's uniqueness and take notice of how you feel when you're with that person.

Enjoy the ride. I'll give as many tips as I can and feel free to reach out to me at www.loveandlaughterlifecoaching.com if you'd like a life coach or a dating consultant to help you navigate the single's world. I coach many clients over the phone so don't think you have to be local for me to be your coach.

My Story

I'LL BEGIN WITH PRACTICING A little vulnerability and tell you my story. I grew up a minister's daughter (with wonderful parents) in Louisville, Kentucky. I had a fantastic childhood (despite my brothers teaming up on me and relentless teasing). I went away to college at Eastern Kentucky University (four glorious years of fun and friends – and enough studying to keep my grades for the sorority and remain there). After returning, I became an elementary school teacher and married a remarkable man, Wes, and we had a happy marriage with normal ups and downs. I could write another whole book about Wes and our escapades, but currently I'm a 51-year-old widow/single mother of two (now adult) kids.

On September 11, 2005, Wes died of a sudden, massive heart attack. He was with the high school church youth group on the first night back together after summer break. Fortunately, my kids (who were 9 and 11 at the time) were not with him. Several gave him CPR as they waited on the ambulance to arrive and regrettably the high school students had to witness this great man they admired die. He was an All American Dad, a youth leader, a choir member, a tennis/ squash player, a businessman. He loved sports, his God and family and friends. In fact, everyone thought they were his best friend. At the young age of 42, he left this earth and left my kids and me (and family and friends) to figure out life without him. I was not mad at God; instead, I felt His arms wrap around me with each of the 2000+ people at his visitation and funeral. We figured out how to be a family of three, how to have two kids in club soccer, work full time, pay the bills, etc. After a year of being a widow, people asked, "Well, are you ready to date?" (as if that's a magical time for all widows to be ready to date; I guess because I was so young?)

"No!" I cried. "I have to raise these kids and have them turn out okay."

Year two, same question and same answer. In fact, I gained 15 pounds because I subconsciously didn't want other men even looking at me. I had zero interest in dating or even looking at another man.

Year three, all of a sudden, God presented me with someone with whom I fell crazy in love. (You know how divorced people sometimes have a "rebound" relationship? Well, widows/widowers can too). At the time, it didn't feel like a rebound. It felt like true love—and probably was. I was crazy about him and he about me. We got our kids on board (even though we went way too fast), went to church, prayed together and we almost got engaged! But, we were in different places with our future desires, so we needed to part ways. I also very much wanted to provide a stepfather for my kids. It was hard breaking up when I was madly in love, but I knew what he and I needed weren't the same. It was the right thing to do. The beauty was, he taught me I could love again (and it surely felt good so I'm grateful for that relationship and he and I are still great friends today). But, where was I going to go to meet new people? I was a single mom who worked all day (I was a teacher) and was at the soccer field every night (both kids in soccer), not to mention all the other responsibilities on my plate.

I did what many other singles did. I started dating on-line. I thought, "How hard can this be? I'll meet an adorable man, fall in love and live happily ever after, right?" After six months, reality set in. "Wow! This is hard! It's so different the second time around." Many men misrepresented themselves, lied and were not the type of quality men I was looking for. Don't get me wrong—I also met some of the best men I've dated online (I found out later it was *me* who wasn't ready). More about that later.

When I began dating, I was a meeting-and-greeting fool. I bet I met five a week and sometimes even three a day (somehow even between soccer games/tournaments). I'm not sure how I did that because I really tried to balance being out and being present at home (there were definitely sometimes I was gone too much—that is a regret). I would double up and take a date to an event so I could kill two birds with one stone and be home that extra night. Then there was a lot of judgment about that. "Wasn't she just with someone else last month?" A lot of jokes about the "flavor of the week." (More about the judgment in dating in Chapter 13). It was a struggle to balance it all but, in the beginning, I was dating for the wrong reason. That was to find a stepdad for my kids—definitely the wrong reason. Fortunately, no one stuck and I was learning a lot about dating the second time around. Wow! Was it/is it ever different! Much of this book will include all that learning, coupled with the books I've read, experts I've spoken to and hundreds of individual conversations with singles.

Over time, I did see a pattern in my dating. Many men were falling in love with me and I wasn't falling back. I mean these men were everything I ever wanted "on paper," but I was just missing what I called "clarity from God" as to whether they were "The One" or not. After noticing this pattern, and recognizing *I* was the common denominator in these relationships, I finally went to therapy (something I should have done after Wes died, but I was too busy taking care of my kids' needs). Unbeknownst to me, I *was* stuck on "loss of Wes" issues and that was why I was pushing everyone away. It was subconscious and I didn't even know it was there. I worked hard with my therapist for about a year to move me to a place of being ready. This is a lesson (for divorced or widow/ers): even though you don't think you need therapy, you just might. At least consider it. Depending on how your spouse died, or how your marriage ended, there are many emotions that need to be processed and it's best to deal with these with a professional.

Also in the midst of dating and discovering, I accidentally started what has become the largest single's group in Louisville, Singles Meet Singles, LLC. It was accidental because I only planned on having one party to connect all these great men I had met with my sweet, single girlfriends. Details about that in Chapter 12. It's a great story and one that I'm happy happened. I'll explain how to start your own single's group if you're interested.

After I retired from a successful, award-winning 27-year teaching career, I decided to go into life coaching. When I did my training with CTI (Coaches Training Institute), they encouraged us to pick a "niche." Something we knew a lot about, something we loved at which we were good and/or about which we were passionate. I picked working with singles since it was "where I was serving." That was how I became a dating consultant. Again, not a matchmaker, or "Hitch," but I use coaching to get at deeper dating issues and try to move singles forward. Many singles just need hope as well as strategies to get to a better (more positive) place. It's easy to spiral down to a dark and negative place. (Are you in a dark, negative place? Let's change that!)

I hosted a radio show for 13 weeks, a show called Love and Laughter. It was a call-in show about relationships: Singles, Marrieds and Friendships. More than anything else, it was a life experience for me. My favorite shows, of course, were the ones with national relationship experts. I learned a lot from them and now I'm here, sharing with you. So let's dive in.

Chapter 1

WHAT? DATING? HOW DO I KNOW WHEN I'M READY?

GREAT QUESTION. WE'RE ALL IN different places with dating: newly divorced and like a kid in the candy store; widowed or divorced for years and ready to settle down; never married and out of a serious, long term relationship; don't want to remarry and every place in between. In fact, one week you might think you're ready and the next you're sure you're nowhere near ready. What to do?

First, it's best that you heal emotionally from your break-up/divorce before jumping back in. Why? Because you're totally not emotionally ready to give 100% to someone else. You'll THINK you are ready. You'll find yourself missing the physical touch and you'll look in all the wrong places to find it (it's not hard to find, by the way!) We'll explore breaking up in Chapter 11, but this chapter will focus on knowing when you're ready to get back out there (either after a divorce, death of a spouse or break up with a boyfriend/girlfriend). I'm talking here about emotionally being ready to jump into a relationship. Does that mean if you're not emotionally ready, you can't date casually? No. You can. But, be clear that that's where you are. If two people are in the same place with dating, it won't be a problem (meaning both wanting to make new friends/date casually—no sex!) But, if you have one emotionally healed person, dating someone who is just starting to heal, you won't be in the same place. Don't pretend to be healed/over your ex if you're really not. More people get hurt when that happens and you may have to deal with another break up (and back to spiraling to that dark, negative place).

Some ask, "What does it mean to be emotionally available?" It means being over your ex/old girl/boyfriend to the point thinking of him/her doesn't evoke tears, anger, resentment or any negative emotion. There are many ways to heal: therapy (*always* a good option), pray, go to church, read a self-help book (so many good ones out there), go out with your girlfriends/guy friends, pamper yourself, reflect, write, meditate, take a class (especially a dating class, if you can find one), hire a life coach and, when you're ready, maybe even a dating consultant.

You might be thinking *how* do I heal?

First, I know it sounds cliché, but do you love yourself? You need to be sure you're grounded in yourself (have taken a long enough break between relationships) and have a healthy perspective for dating. Do you think you're a desirable, positive, happy person? If you said yes, you may be ready. If you answered no, here a few suggestions (these are also good when you are trying to get over the one with whom you broke up):

- Go to church—get spiritually healthy. Ask God (or your higher power) to help lead and guide you along the way. To help heal you from the inside out.

- Examine your values and decide WHO you want to be in the dating world—then become that person. Andy Stanley (minister at North Point Community Church in Alpharetta) says, "Are you who the one you're looking for is looking for?" This is such great advice. If you're a party girl and sleeping with every man in sight (or party boy doing the same), yet you don't want to marry someone like that, the man (or woman) you ultimately want to marry is not like that, s/he won't even *see* you or look your way. Be the person you're looking for is looking for. He says, "Instead of searching for the right person, become the right person."

- Hire a dating coach/consultant.

- Don't date to fill an empty heart or get over your ex or save your dreadful life. You won't find dating fun if you're in this place and you won't be a good partner to the other person. You need to find ways to become WHOLE on your own first before you can give yourself to someone else.

- Read some dating books—there are so many good ones out there. You've started with a good one here and I'll recommend some others throughout this book and in Chapter 14.

- Spend time with positive people. Catch yourself when you're being negative and turn negative statements into positives.
- Hit the gym. Get physically healthy.
- Start a new project.
- Spend time away from your computer by going outdoors. Nothing clears a mind like being in nature.
- Do activities that bring you joy.
- Read self-help books or the Bible. Join a Bible study.
- Go to therapy to clear things from your past. A lot of times we don't even know we are "stuck" so it's important to explore and get a "check up" from the "neck up."
- Volunteer/serve in your community.
- Take your nieces and nephews out to the zoo or park. Enjoy laughing with young minds.
- Travel some place you've never been.
- Some people say make a list of what you're looking for. You can do this, but know that that list very well may change again and again. I mean yes, we all want someone who is loyal, honest, has good character, but don't make your list so constrictive that no one can match it (i.e. "I only want to date someone who is 6'-6'2" with blonde hair, likes music and makes $150,000+"). It's more about the way you FEEL when you're with this person. I'm not talking crazy chemistry/infatuation/lustful feelings. I'm talking about through a lot of conversation you can see this

person would be a good match for you (no matter what your list says).

A Quick List of 10 Ways to Know If You're Ready to Date Again

1. You've Rediscovered Who You Are

Whether you're a widow/er or divorced, you need to rediscover who you are without your partner. What type of activities do you like now that you're single? Maybe try a few things you've not been able to try before (because you were not single).

2. Guilty Feelings are Gone

Widow/ers might feel this more because you didn't ask to be single. We are all wired for connection, but it might feel funny going out again so soon. As soon as the guilty feelings are gone, it's a sign you're ready.

3. You Feel Like the Rest of Your Life is Stable

It's important (and responsible) to not feel shaky about other areas of your life (finances, job, kids, etc.). This doesn't mean you have to wait until life is perfect (that'll never happen), but you should not be treading water each day keeping up with your responsibilities.

4. No More Negative Feelings

If you had a tough divorce, it'll take time to get rid of the anger, bitterness and even revengeful feelings. This is something people in general always have to work on! It's so easy to go to negative places—just don't live there. Find ways to pull yourself out of it. Living in the state of gratitude is a great way! Surround yourself with positive people (and stay away from the ones who help you spiral down).

5. No Comparisons to the Past

It's probably not a good idea to talk often about how wonderful your deceased husband was or how great your marriage was when it was good. A little bit of that is okay, but if you're talking a lot about your past (especially early on), then your current date might think they're being compared. Comparisons to past girlfriends/boyfriends will not go over well. Look for the uniqueness of the one you're with (remember you would not like to be compared to past partners, either).

6. Ready to Be Vulnerable Again

If you were cheated on or hurt in a past relationship, it might be hard to trust again. You will get better at setting boundaries (defining boundaries as well as protective boundaries). But eventually, you'll need to work through those issues (therapy?) so you can be vulnerable and trust again. It is a big risk to put yourself out there again, but that is part of the process. Each relationship makes you stronger for the next. And because God wired us for relationships, we must remain open to what/who is best for us.

7. Free of Fear

No matter the age, we're all fearful of something: "He won't like me because I'm too fat"; "She won't like me because I'm balding." The older we get, the sooner we learn that we're enough just the way we are. Find ways to *not* live in fear. Seize opportunities that come your way (scary as they may be). The man or woman that falls in love with you will love you for all the reasons others didn't!

8. You'll Be Dating for the Right Reasons

You won't be dating for the kids, to find a stepparent, for remorse over your ex or to fill a lonely heart. You'll be ready to date to enhance *your* life; not to *complete you*, but to *complement* you.

9. You're Finished Grieving

Widow/ers obviously will grieve, but divorced people will too. Grieving the loss of a marriage of however many years is also tough. There will be many raw emotions that need to be processed. Given time, healing does occur. You can't change what happened to you, but you can choose how you react to it.

10. You'll be Excited to Date

You'll experience the anticipation of that first kiss; taking longer to get ready for your date; butterflies and being a little nervous (just like in high school). It'll just feel like it's the right time. You might meet the wrong person, but the process will feel right.

I tell my clients that dating is 90% timing, meaning you have to be in the right place at the right time, have similar values and character, to be able to live with each other's baggage, have similar faith, you happen to live somewhat close to each other, are able to meet the other's communication needs, both be emotionally available and have physical attraction... oh yeah, all this has to go both ways! So, it's 90% timing and 99% of the ones you meet will not be the one. Only one makes it in the end.

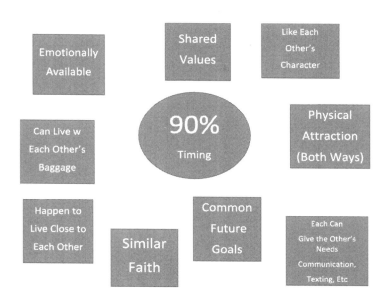

Okay. Now you're feeling more whole. You've done the work. You're emotionally, spiritually, physically healthy and you're ready to go. Congratulations. Yikes! Where do you go? What do you do?

Reflection Questions:

After reading this chapter, do you think you're ready? What things make you know you're ready or not?

_____

_____

_____

_____

_____

_____

Chapter 2
I THINK I'M READY

IF YOU'RE NEW TO THE dating world, you'll soon find out it is *very* different than round one when you were younger or in your 20's. We have had a lot of life experiences that make us more cautious. We have been burned by bad decisions by either us or our partners. Sometimes we're told that we're "less than" and need to rediscover who we are. We now have children and their needs come before anyone we date. That whole 90% timing mentioned in Chapter 1 is real.

If you have young children, it's going to be hard to date. Divorced people have every other weekend and widows have kids 24/7. You can try to dabble and meet people in hopes that he also has his kids the same weekend as you, but it's just very hard. Not impossible, just hard. Plus *don't* lose your focus in raising kids. It's the most important job God entrusted to us, so even though we are all hardwired for connection and we all want to love and be loved, try to keep the main thing the main thing. If you're organized and resourceful, you certainly can date while rearing children. (As your children get older and can stay by themselves and drive, it'll get much easier).

Where to go when you're ready to date? Let's start with some...

<u>Off Line Options:</u>

- Go to where people are (park, museum, festivals, etc.), not a movie or comedy club. You can't engage and talk to people there.
- Tell your friends you're ready to date and ask if they know anyone. I know—a blind date? Well, you'll probably ask to see his/her picture first (good idea) *and* ask some basic questions about them (good idea). But remember, it's just a meet. It's *not* a commitment to marriage or even a second date. It's just to get out there and meet people (more about that in Chapter 8 under different perspectives in dating).
- Say yes to all invitations (from co-workers, church, old college friends, etc.). Remain open.
- Attend church and church activities regularly.
- Go to the gym.
- Start a single's group (I'll teach you how in Chapter 12).
- Join or form a wine tasting or dining club.
- Try a single's cruise. You may meet people too far away to date, but you're getting out there and meeting other singles traveling the same path as you. You'll make good friendship connections with people all over the world.

- Go to "target rich" places where there's plethora of people (sporting events, flea markets, auctions, game watching parties).
- Organize a Girl's Night Out or Guy's Night Out. Through friends, you meet friends.
- Make a Facebook event for your friends to meet up at Happy Hour after work on a Thursday or Friday.
- Go rock climbing or hiking.
- Go to networking events.
- Hang out in book stores.
- Participate in salsa nights.
- Join a cooking class, acting class, etc.

How to Look Available?

- The #1 thing you can do is *smile*! Show your teeth and smile up through your eyes!
- When you see someone you like, look at him/her. Make eye contact. Look away. Look back at him/her and smile. That is one way to let the other know you're open to conversation and approachable. (This is flirting 101). I did not include much about body language in this book, but there are many great videos and books on this topic. It's quite fascinating. Brush up on learning about body language and flirting.
- If you're with a group of girls, don't make a circle where no man would even want to approach. Make a semi-circle or just gather with two-three girls. Not

a huge group. Women are not approachable by men if in a big group.

- Take your jacket off as if to say you're staying a while; hold your head high and shoulders back.
- Stand, don't sit.
- Be friendly to *everyone*. (A great way to practice putting positivity in the world).
- Put your phone away! Staring at your phone does NOT make you approachable (I know it's a security blanket for some).
- Laugh and talk to everyone.
- Touch people when you're talking (arm, hand, shoulder).

I think it's best if you let a man approach you. That's how you know he's really interested. However, if you're a woman and want to be bold, you can always say:

1. Hey, I like your shoes. Did you get those at _____?
2. Did I meet you through _____ (friend's name) maybe at _____ (location)?
3. Don't you work with _____ (friend's name) at _____ (company)?
4. Can you help me _____ (figure something out, where to find, etc.)?

Sometimes men are shy to approach and they just need a reason to talk to you. Once you start (and *if* they're interested), they will take it from there.

How do you know if he's into you? (Some body language included here).

- He'll smile.
- His shoulders will be back and will stand tall.
- He'll expand (alpha male move- cross legs, put arms around chair, puff out his chest, taking up more space).
- He'll touch his face.
- He'll lean in.
- His belly button/torso and feet will face toward you.
- He'll find ways to touch you (arm, hand).
- He'll text and call you and pursue!
- Let him initiate! If he likes you, you'll hear from him. There is nothing you can do to make him stop. If he's not, you won't hear as much from him (or you'll get short answers) and there's nothing you can do to make him like you.

Reflection Questions:

What of these things listed resonate with you? Where are the best offline options for you?

Chapter 3

ONLINE DATING

As YOU MAY KNOW, THERE are a lot of statistics about the success rate of online connections and relationships (Right now it's one in five couples meet online, but it'll likely change and be higher by the time this book is published; online dating is here to stay). Dating online used to be taboo, but not anymore. It's a quite popular and acceptable way to meet new people (especially for the 35+ age group). I would approach online dating with the attitude that you're just going to meet new friends.

Let's face it: *most* of the ones you meet (unfortunately) will not be "The One." Only one lucky man/woman makes it in the end. So that means the one you're meeting tonight will not likely be the one. So just have fun. Enjoy the ride. Look at it as an adventure and a learning process. Because the VALUE of dating is LEARNING. Learning what you like and don't like. Things you thought were important really might not be and vice versa. Learning how to let someone down easily, learn how to flirt, how to set boundaries, how to practice vulnerability, the list goes on. In the beginning, it might be good to "Date to Date" (more on that perspective in Chapter 8 under different perspectives in dating) instead of "Date to Mate."

When I speak to groups of people about online dating I explain that...

<u>Dating is Like a Consignment Shop:</u>

- When you walk in the consignment shop (online site) and look at all the racks of clothes (people), your first thought is WOW. Look at all these clothes (men/women). So many choices. Surely I'll find something (someone) I'll like.

- As you start looking though the racks, you find that most don't look like your type. You might say, "No way! Oh gross! Not in a million years! Eww! No way would I EVER put that on my body!" (Translation: No way would I go out with or even meet that person. I'm not at all attracted. Really? No teeth? Fifteen fishing pictures, too tall/short/young/old, etc.). We all have our preferences. There's nothing wrong with that. It's a good thing we don't all have or like the same look. Just remember that there is a human being behind that profile. They are all looking for love like you.

- Every now and then, we find one outfit that looks good. "Hmmmm... I might try on that one." (Translation: The wink, send a message, do you like me? I think I like you).

- We put that outfit over our arm and *keep looking* through the rack because we're not sure how it'll fit us (Translation: We have to keep looking and stay available because we're not sure how that last item/person will fit).

- Eventually we go try on the outfits. (Translation: I call this the meet-n- greet: when you go and meet for the first time). I suggest trying on (talking to) three to four at a time and not 19-20. It gets a little overwhelming if you try to juggle too many.

- We usually know right away if it is a good fit or not. If it's not, we put it back on the rack. That outfit will fit someone else better. It's a nice outfit, just not good for me. (Translation: S/he wasn't my type, but he'll/she'll be a good fit for someone else because there's someone for everyone).

- If we are not totally sure—"Well, I think this outfit looks okay on me. I'm not sure how it'd go with my shoes or purse." (Translation: Will he like my kids? Will she fit into where I am with my life?) So we buy it and see how it looks over time. (Translation: Another date. Go out again and see how it feels to be with this new person. Are we in the same place in our lives?)

- Over time we see how well that outfit is made (Translation: Upbringing/baggage) Is it falling apart? Poorly made? (Translation: Did his momma teach him manners? Did she learn lessons on how to be a sweet, kind lady?) Some are definitely better made than others. We usually like those that were made similar to us (common values, character, upbringing, etc.).

- We see how we feel while wearing it (Translation: How we feel with him, how he treats her). Is it versatile in all seasons? (Observe through every season).

- We might need to resell that outfit to the shop because it didn't look as good as you thought it did. Back to the rack it goes because it'll be good for someone. Still a nice outfit. (Translation: After dating him/her you see that s/he is a nice person, but not going to be a forever match/fit).

- Each week, new clothes come in to the shop so it's important to go back and look (Translation: There are always newly divorced/widowed/available men/women. Stay online and/or stay out there. Stay available to be found).

- You might even try a different consignment shop: upscale, down home, best prices (Translation: different internet sites/different offerings/different people).

- You may ask, "Why even shop? It's SO much work. Most of the items are either junk or don't fit right or are too old looking, etc. It takes forever to find just one item worth trying on." (Translation: Why work so hard to find a good match? It's so hard to find a good fit).

- The answer is because we eventually find that *golden nugget/gem* that fits JUST RIGHT! (Translation: This is "The One." The one we can live with forever. It looks good on us. It's well made. It looks good with our accessories and has lasted and looks good in every season).

- It's worth it because shopping (dating) is fun and the right outfit makes us feel good and the best ones last forever! (If dating isn't fun, you probably need to take a break).

If you're really ready to date, keep your profile up until you go exclusive with someone. Don't just join for a month and say, "Well, I tried that and didn't meet anyone or I only met creeps!" Yes, you may meet some creeps or not nice people. *Stay on* (if you truly want to date). The longer you do it the quicker you find out how to refine your matches and meets. You'll get better at reading people. Stay on, even years, if it's assisting you with getting new meets/dates. It's a great way to meet new people. It's not the *only* way, just one way to find others in your age range. So stay online, and do all the other things listed in Chapter 1.

Which Site is Right?

This is where a dating coach can help you and/or someone who has dated online for a while. It's a personal preference and your age might be a part of picking the right one for you. There are many sites and apps available, but here are the most popular and well known, as of this writing:

1. Zoosk
2. Match.com
3. eHarmony
4. Plenty of Fish
5. EliteSingles
6. JDate (for Jewish singles)
7. Black People Meet
8. OurTime.com
9. Christian Mingle
10. How About We
11. SingleParentMeet
12. Millionaire Match
13. Tinder (app)
14. OK Cupid (app)
15. Bumble (app)

Some of these are paid sites and some are free. You'll find that on a site that asks for a subscription, people tend to be looking for something more serious. They're more likely to actually move from behind the screen to meet and there are less abusive and/or sexual messages. But they're not for everyone. People just wanting to dip their toes into the pool for the purpose of looking around might start with a free site. Maybe they don't want to invest much time and energy into a serious relationship; therefore, they don't want to work on making a complete, quality profile. There are a lot of fish in the sea and many different oceans or swimming pools in which to swim. It totally depends on your purpose in dating.

*NOTE: If you're not a techie person, don't let online dating scare you away. There are many people that can teach you how to use the Internet. Once you have a few lessons, you won't believe how easy it is. It's part of dating in this century. Definitely don't let that be your excuse for not dating online. (You used to not know how to drive a car. Or bake a cake. It's an easy learn).

Pros and Cons of Internet Dating—there are a great deal of opinions on this, but here are the main pros and cons...

PROS:
- It's a great way to meet new people you would never otherwise meet at work or on the street.
- They provide a good screening process. Assuming everyone is telling the truth, you can quickly find out age, education, kids, smoker, drinker, faith, etc. You can also tell a little about their personality and sense of humor by their writing.

- It saves time. You can go to one site and find all the ones in your age range that are also single and available.

- It's safe in that you don't have to give your name or number if you don't want.

- No more stigma with online dating and no more bars! (And you can "window shop" in your pajamas).

- It's definitely a great way to jump back into dating. Dating online is just a resource to help you with meeting other singles. There are no guarantees you'll find "The One," but it's a great way to meet new people on your same path (and, of course, you hope to find "The One").

- There are a slew of options. Not only on one site, but if you have a profile on a few sites, you may see double the people you can view. If you're ready to date, you should be having meets if you're online.

- The sites are relatively inexpensive and there are many free ones. (Being free can also be a con. You get what you pay for! So beware).

- The fear of rejection is reduced. If a man/woman isn't interested, it's best to be rejected by someone you don't even know yet.

CONS:

- You're not totally sure who is behind that profile. It takes some practice to know which ones are fake profiles and which are real people. It can sometimes attract perverts, weirdos or creeps (this is increased with the free sites). A dating coach or someone who has dated a long time online can help you recognize these types. The longer you're online, the better "read" of these types you'll be.

- In the beginning it's addictive and time consuming. You need to watch your time when online. You'll never get that time back! Maybe after your first week, limit your online time to one hour a day.

- It's overwhelming when you first get on. A lot of winks and messages. Everyone always wants to talk to the new people online. (Of course, this can also be flattering and therefore a pro).

- Some just are looking for a pen pal. The goal is to actually meet and date!

- Some sites ask for way too much money. Probably best to go for a middle of the road one to get your feet wet (I don't recommend only free sites if you're serious about finding "The One"). The free sites are okay for maybe getting your feet wet, and maybe in addition to a paid site, but the majority of people on the free sites and apps are not always fully invested. With the paid sites, people seem more invested because they have to spend time filling out a profile and pay money to participate. (Please don't take this as me saying there are only bad people, sex maniacs and creeps on the free sites. There are nice people there, too. I have, at one point in time, tried them all. I'm just broad stroking in comparison to the paid sites).

- It can be frustrating. Someone may be talking to you and all of a sudden s/he disappears (usually meaning s/he has more of a connection with someone else). The experts call this "ghosting." I find that honesty is the best policy with all your communications. It's okay to tell where you are with dating. Better to give an honest, "I'm not interested" than the "silent no" and leave someone wondering. I have a few clients that are "pleasers." They say, "I don't want to hurt anyone's feelings." If you're kind and honest, it's up to them to have their feelings hurt or not. That is out of your control. But if you're kind and honest, that's the best thing you can do.

- New people to online dating might get what I call "Match-itus" meaning the first one they go to meet doesn't get a fair shake because they're talking to about five to ten other people. Person #2 is hot; #3 is a great communicator; #4 is in your line of work, etc. So I suggest only juggling about three to four at a time. Sometimes there are too many choices and no one gets a fair shake. Hopefully, over time, one of those will emerge to the top of the pile.

Do's and Don'ts of Internet Dating

I'll make a general list of do's and don'ts. Many dating books will include a list of these. I'm picking the ones I think are most useful...

Do's:

- Have at least one good head shot within the last year. You should be recognizable when you meet! (Those with pictures are 15 times more likely to be viewed).

- Always one full body picture that represents what you really look like right now (in the last year). Update this year to year.

- Be honest with your body type. Are you really average? Slim? Curvy? A "few" extra pounds? Big Beautiful? Fifty pounds is more than a few extra pounds. You are who you are and this category should match your pictures. If you're athletic and toned, declare it. If you *used* to be athletic and toned in college, you can't claim it if that's changed. For every body type, there's someone looking for you. Not everyone wants tall and slim.

- Action pictures are great! Doing things you like to do like a baseball game, concert, beach, sports, bike-riding with your kids.

- SMILE! Show your teeth. Teeth and eyes are big attributes singles look at and like.

- Post at least four pictures (preferably doing things you like to do).

- Mention the most interesting and compelling thing about you. What makes you different? What makes you come alive?

- It's a good idea to have your user name and headline pop out. Positive. Maybe a double play on words. Creative.

- Have fun and learn from each experience! More tips later in this chapter.

- Completely fill out your profile, answering every question (except income). Don't just say, "I'll fill this out later." Actually put time and energy into filling out your profile. I say except income because if you make a lot of money, some are looking for a sugar daddy or momma. If you make $25,000 a year others will judge that's not enough and won't give you a chance. Salary is private and will be made known at the right time when in relationship.

- I was a third grade teacher and one thing I taught my students was "Show, Don't Tell." Don't *tell* how sweet, kind, funny and wonderful you are, *show* them through a story. Paint a picture that after reading, your audience will say, "Wow. She's sweet," or "How funny!"

Don'ts:

- No glamour shots! Yes, you look beautiful and touched up, but we don't look like that every day. Best to show the real, every day you!

- No forced sexuality. You know what I mean. No cleavage for women and no shirts off for men.

- No old photos! You will lose on the first meet if you don't look like your pictures (I love this funny Facebook post I saw that said, "If you don't look like your pictures, you're going to buy the drinks until you do.")

- No party-face. If you're a party girl/boy, probably not flattering to showboat that. It might be a fun picture to you, but scary to others.

- No bathroom mirror shots! Have you ever seen what's behind you? A toilet? One man I saw was standing in front of a condom machine (perhaps that was subliminal.) Find or have made some good pictures of you.

- No long distance pictures. It won't help if the person looking at you can't really see you. (Same goes for blurry pictures).

- No big group photos. They have to work too hard to see which one you are.

- No sunglasses or caps. Again, we can't really see your face. We need to see your eyes and smile for sure!

- No dogs, cars, sunsets, houses without *you* in them. We don't want to date your dog or a sunset or your house.

- Pictures with (older) kids (optional) based on your comfort level. There are a lot of crazies out there, so it totally depends on how you feel about that. If your kids are 17 and 19 and are all over social media anyway, probably won't matter as much. If they're three and five, you don't want their picture to be copied by a porn film agent. I know, sad to even think about.

- Men, please don't post all fishing pictures! Or five motorcycle pictures. One will suffice. Ladies, same goes for your cat! Or your beloved car (or other prized possession). The person viewing you wants to see *you*!

- Don't make a laundry list of perfect girl or guy traits. We, of course, all would love someone who is hot, rich, funny, interesting, travels the world and is an All American parent. Maybe pick your top two-three things you're looking for.

- Don't put a body part or anything sexual in your user name. Am I really having to say this? At least this is a good screening process for some. It'll help you skip over these profiles. (For example, "goindown69," "sexkitten," etc.—I've read worse). You get the picture. (Sorry to insult the intelligence of most of the singles reading this. But, sometimes people are given bad advice from their buddies.)

- Don't get too romantic. Every woman wants a romantic man, but if you get too mushy with your words, you sound disingenuous.
- No bad mouthing your ex or past relationship (i.e. "Divorce #2 so now I'm another statistic," or "Why do I always attract the psychos?") Instead say something like, "I'm going to give this online dating a try and hoping to meet some wonderful people."

Your Profile Summary:

This is an important piece of your profile because it's where your personality can shine through. Yes, your pictures can also do that, but can you write a complete sentence? Do you have positive or negative energy? Does your sense of humor leap off the page? Here are some common tips:

- What is your purpose in dating? Casual dating? New friends? Committed relationship? Marriage-minded? If you post what you think men or women want to read, how do you really know what they want? They want different things just like we do. I personally am marriage-minded, so knowing someone is newly divorced and is just looking for casual dating or a sexual relationship, I know we won't have the same purpose in dating. This definitely saves time with weeding out non-matches (and saves you time from meeting them).

- Beware of clichés. "Looking to spoil the lady of my dreams with flowers and candlelight," "I enjoy walks on the beach in the moonlight," or "Looking for my knight in shining armor." Another common one: "Looking for my soul mate." None of these is unique. Practically every man and woman likes and wants those things. Be different. SHOW, don't tell. Telling is: "I'm a very caring, sweet, professional woman with two kids and one grandbaby." You just described 75% of my 50-year-old female friends. Instead, add emotion. "The highlight of my Saturday is coming home to my two-year-old grandson running my direction, knocking me down with his hugs and kisses," or, "After we have dated a while, I can see us cooking while dancing in the kitchen and singing into the stirring spoons." Why not talk about the zip-lining trip you took in Costa Rica? How did it feel to conquer your first marathon? Think about what makes you tick.

- Don't go by profile pictures alone. There is a human being behind that profile. As you become older, the smaller your pool of candidates gets. If the person sitting across from you is kind, give him/her another chance. You may not have crazy sparks flying across the table, but sometimes that grows over time (and if it doesn't, then at least you gave him/her a second chance).

- Real men lose their hair and have love handles.

- Real women have curves and wrinkles.
- Take out anything negative. If you include phrases like, "Players, cheaters, liars, etc. pass me on by," "Drama queens, pass me by," or "If you're not over your ex or and you're not emotionally available, swipe left." This shows you've had these issues in the past, or have been burned by such people, and it sounds negative. Tell what you do want, not what you don't want. This is why it's important to have a few friends read your profile. You want to see if it reads as positive and tells (or shows) who you truly are.
- Men want a woman who has feminine energy, someone that will not be a threat or burden. Women want a man with masculine energy that will provide and protect.
- No one wants to date someone who is needy or lacks confidence. Confidence is the most attractive quality. Neediness is the least attractive.
- Don't lie about your age, height or weight. Hey, how about don't lie about anything? As soon as someone lies to you, there is a doubt in your mind as to what else will they might lie about. Lying will never benefit you.
- Education is important to many so don't leave that off, but do leave off your income, especially if you make a lot of money. You want people contacting

you because of you and not because of the amount of money you make. There are plenty looking for a sugar daddy or sugar momma.

- Keep refining your profile over time. Every time you make a change, you go back to the top of the pile with the site's algorithm. I'd suggest changing your primary picture once a week and about once a month refine your summary.

- I tell my clients to read 20-40 profiles (of the same sex) before writing your own. See what everyone else is including and don't include that (i.e., "I like a woman who can put on a pair of jeans and a cap then put on her little black dress and go to a black tie event.") Many say this. Be different.

- A general rule of thumb for length is about two to three paragraphs. Make it show you put some effort in to it, but if it's too long, not all will take the time to read it!

- CHECK YOUR SPELLING AND GRAMMAR! Then check it again. Have a friend read it. Again, keep refining (and making it accurate). For example, if you've been online dating for four years, be sure to change the kids' ages, your pictures to keep them current and perhaps you've had a career change.

- TIP: The best time to be online is Sunday nights from 6:00-9:00 p.m.

Reflection Questions:

What is your opinion of online dating? After reading this, has it changed? If so, how? If not, what reservations do you still have?

Communicating Online

Now you have your profile, your pictures look great and you've fully filled out the site's questions (it is important to have a complete profile. Otherwise, it'll look like you didn't put much time or effort into it. That might equal the time and effort you'll put into your next relationship). It's time to start talking to people. Many experts and your friends will have different opinions and advice about the way to go about this, but these are my suggestions.

Remember, the goal is to eventually meet the person behind the screen to see if s/he would be a good match for you. Here are the most common questions I get about the "how to's" of online dating:

1. I hear about fake profiles. How do I know which ones are fake?

For a woman, a man's fake profile usually has these common characteristics: the men are incredibly good looking, most claim to be a widower, usually one child, usually not a ton of pictures, claim to make $150+, career is many times labor/construction. When emailing, their English will be broken, their message very long with sappy "Looking for my soulmate and distance doesn't matter" type talk. Many will say, "I don't come to this site much, please find me on ***yahoo IM." They might also be "currently out of the country." After that (if they can hook you in) they may ask for money. Don't let it get that far. Look for the signs early on (your gut might tell you this doesn't sound like how a normal man talks). Also, sometimes their profile will only be open for a few days and then *poof* will be gone. (This goes for women and men).

For men: Usually on a woman's fake profile, the ladies are 30-35, never married, no kids, very pretty, usually out of your state, minimum summary, one-two pictures and don't have much to say. They also will have broken English. If you watch for a few days, you'll see their profiles don't stay up long. Those of us that are good at recognizing fake profiles report them and they're taken down.

2. How do I know if someone is lying to me?

This takes time to learn, just like in real life. People don't lie because they're online, they lie because it's a character flaw. Most lie because they think you won't like them just the way they are (because they're too short or too old or over weight). You could meet a woman at a bar that's married and she lies saying she's single. So the discovery about this is about the same.

If it moves from online to texting, ask, "What is your last name for my phone? Mine is _____." Then you can search them (not friend) on Facebook and/or LinkedIn. Sometimes you can match their high school or college graduation date with his/her age. See if the two match. Of course, if you have common friends, you can ask for a character reference (I'd only ask if it's someone you know well. It might be his old girl-friend you're asking or his cousin in which case s/he will run back to tell the person someone is stalking them, and kindly give your name). This might sound like stalking to some, but especially as a woman, you want to find out if this person is safe and a good guy in their eyes (of course, the good guy part you'll want to find out on your own but there's nothing wrong with finding out if s/he is a safe person). I googled one guy I was talking to and I found out he beat his ex-wife and was put in jail. I'd probably rather know that before meeting than after!

Now, because you're searching them, know that they're also probably searching you. Clean up what you don't want to be seen. Set high security settings on your Facebook if you have a problem with people checking you out. Or if you have nothing to hide, being public isn't a big deal. It's personal preference. Some say, "I'd just rather go and meet him or her and find out on my own." There is nothing wrong with that way of thinking (until later you find out you have 30 friends in common and they all knew that he cheated on his wife and is really only separated and not divorced yet). But, yes, do what is comfortable for you. Some things are worth checking out in advance. You will learn what feels best for you over time. Now, if someone says, "Oh, he's a player" or "I think he's weird" or "She's high maintenance." Those types of things are good for you to figure out on your own. "Player" is an over-used term that we'll discuss in Chapter 13, and the other comments are opinions. Don't let someone's opinion stop you from at least meeting a new friend.

3. Do I have to respond to everyone? What if I'm not attracted?

This will totally be up to you but I'll give you my opinion: if someone speaks to you on the street or at a party, do you ignore him/her or say hello back? Saying hello to someone doesn't mean you're interested in going on a date. I think it's polite to respond (I'm talking about messages, not winks. If someone winks at me on the street, I don't always wink back). Most of your messages will be letting them know you're not interested. Some say, "That's mean. I don't want to hurt anyone's feelings." It hurts much more to get a "silent no."

So here is what I say (I even have this in a short cut in my phone so all I have to do is type three letters and this whole message types out). "Thanks for reaching out. I don't think we're a match but I wish you luck and love." Then I sign my first name. Most who get this reply with a big THANK YOU for responding (which tells me most don't bother replying). Some will be offended and say, "Really? How can you know if we haven't even met?" My response is, "Please don't take it personally. We all have our preferences in what/who we are looking for. You seem like a very sweet man. I'm sorry and good luck." If s/he continues messaging or starts being mean, block!

4. Should I wink and run or send a message?

It's always better to send a message. Winking and running are for amateurs and scaredey-cats. (Also, non-paying members might be able to wink but not send or receive messages. This varies by the site). It's best to pick out something from their profile that stands out to you and comment and/or ask a question. Women and men can usually tell when a message has been copied and pasted, so don't do that. Be unique if you're really interested. Never just say, "Hi" or "Hi sexy." I'd say you don't have to respond to those because they're not putting much effort into messaging you. (Men, don't call women sexy when you don't know them. It has an air of "I want to have sex with you." It's a safer thing to say when you're already dating someone).

5. Who should initiate the message?

As Wendy Walsh (relationship expert) says, "Sperm chases egg." It's always best for the man to initiate a date (otherwise, the woman doesn't know how interested he is). It would be best if they initiate online, too, but some are new to online dating and are not sure what to do or say. One tip might be to view his profile so he can see that you viewed. If he in turn views you and you don't hear from him, he may not be interested (or isn't a paying member yet). Or you can "like" one of his pictures (to prompt him to view you). But, I also think this is appropriate: if I see a person in the grocery store or at a party, many times I'll initiate with, "Hi" or "I'm Elizabeth." I'll know pretty quickly if the man is interested because of the way he engages in conversation. So for the very *first* message (only), I think it is okay to also pick something out of his profile on which to comment and keep it short and sweet. Something like, "Hey there. I also have a son that goes to UK. Would you look at my profile and let me know if there's any interest?" If they view you and you don't hear from them, they're not interested so don't continue messaging.

Remember to not take it personally. There are many perfectly normal, good people that just won't be attracted to you (or you to them) just because of their preferences and past experiences. If they are interested, they'll message you back and *then* you can let him pursue. All you did was initiate a conversation just like you would do at a party. After that party, you're going to let him pursue, ask for your number and ask you out. You just made him notice you. This goes against the "rules" book, but there are just too many options out there, so I think it's just a way of saying, "Look at my profile. What do you think?"

6. I read a book and it said to wait 24 hours before responding. Should I really wait an entire day to respond?

That more than likely came from the book *The Rules for Online Dating* (which is a great book full of a lot of great ideas. I think it's worth a read). That was written in the context of you wait to respond because you have a full life that's busy and mysterious and you don't want to appear to be too eager. I agree with that except with today's technology, when we are sent notifications of when someone messages us, I think it's okay to reply by the end of the day—not right away. Not in the first 30 seconds or even minutes of his email. But, I think if he sends an email at 9:00 a.m., you can respond after work or before bedtime and not appear too eager. The same goes for Tinder and other apps. They all immediately notify you when someone writes you. Don't respond right away. Otherwise, it'll look like you're sitting online just waiting for him to message (not a full life). If you want to wait 24 hours, that's okay too. I think you should only spend an hour a day online (instead of all day or hours each day). Otherwise, it gets to be overwhelming; you end up juggling too many meets and you can't get that time back.

What if you don't have a full life? Get one!

Remember that men are hunters. Let them hunt. They love the chase/challenge. A good rule of thumb is to wait to respond twice as long as it took him to respond to you. They actually may think more about you when you don't respond right away. They might wonder what you are up to. If you find this hard to do (as do I) keep a journal close by and respond there. Or email yourself the response. Then after you wait a bit, just copy and paste what you wrote to yourself and hit send. (Many times you might change your mind with your response because you paused long enough to actually *think* about your response). Novel idea, right? Actually *thinking* before responding?

7. How long do I email before we meet?

For me, long enough to know he can write a complete sentence (and sound real). But not long enough to be a pen pal and go nowhere. Evan Marc Katz (a dating coach) says the connection feels good when you have two emails on the site, two emails off the site, two phone calls and then meet. *The Rules for Online Dating* book says: if a man hasn't asked you out by four emails, move on. You obviously have to do what feels right, but make sure you're moving forward and not just "chit chatting." The goal of online dating is to step away from the computer and actually meet. If you think you are sure enough about the person on the other side of the profile, you can say, "I've enjoyed chatting with you on here, but I think I'd like to have coffee and actually meet the face behind the computer. The worst thing that can happen is we meet a new friend. Thoughts?"

In my early days of online dating, there were several men (a few of which were out of town) that were great emailers! Very attentive, detail-oriented, and they said all the right things that resonated with me. Our conversations flowed. I'm the type that can fall in love with words. After a while, there was this false sense of being in relationship after having a lot of online talking but never meeting. I totally got my hopes up about these men. Then when I met them, I felt nothing. No attraction at all and I learned to not email so much as to not get wrapped up in words. You know *nothing* until you meet face to face.

I will suggest for the long distance men/women, after a few emails and you sense initial attraction, actually Facetime or Skype before meeting. It'll give you a sense of who they are before actually traveling to meet. (This can save a lot of time and money!)

8. How personal should I get? Where I work? Live?

Again this is personal preference as to how much you share, but I would not give any specifics until you meet them. Again, you need to see who is behind that screen before divulging too much. If someone asked where I taught (I was a teacher), I'd say an elementary school in Jefferson County. Or where do you live? I live in the east end. You can be as vague as you need to be. If you feel uncomfortable, you can simply say, "I don't share that until I actually meet and know someone." That answer should be respected (and will hopefully urge him to ask you to meet).

9. What if I'm not attracted to the person after our meet-n-greet?

For me, this is like telling someone online you're not interested. In fact, now that you've met the person, I think it's rude to not reply with something. This individual made an extra effort to leave a full and busy life to come and meet you (as did you) and a reply is kind. No one wants to hurt anyone's feelings. So don't give the "silent no." Again, no one likes the silent no. Do you? (Golden Rule?) With a silent no, you're replaying the date in your mind trying to figure out what s/he like or was it something you said. More than likely, the attraction wasn't there or maybe you each have different goals in life. Here is my standard answer I give if I'm not feeling it:

"Thanks so much for the coffee. I enjoyed my time but, I was only feeling friendship. I'd certainly enjoy being friends."

Or, "Thanks for dinner. I didn't feel any electricity shooting across the table. I surely hope we can still be friends."

Or for me since I organize a single's group (or if you're part of a single's group, you can do the same). "I was only feeling friendship, but I have this great single's group I could add you to on Facebook. Because you're a decent man/woman, I'd totally be okay with introducing you to my other single friends. This group is a great place to make new friends and maybe through friends, you will meet your next Mr./Mrs. Right?"

These are just a few examples. The important thing is you're honest. Don't keep texting and communicating often if you're not feeling it because that leaves the one on the other end hopeful. You can be kind and honest. Remember, most of them will not be a match anyway. But, maybe your next Mr./Mrs. Right is that person's best friend.

10. How long do I/we keep our profiles up after we start dating?

I think you both keep your profiles up until there is a conversation about being exclusive (which means let's only date each other to see where we go). Until that conversation, there should be no "assuming" you're exclusive and not meeting others. If you have sex before this conversation, you're leaving yourself open for hurts or complications. Once you've decided to go offline, it's okay to just "close" your profile (as opposed to canceling). Within a few months, you'll know how solid you are and if you'd like to keep seeing this person. The important thing is that you stay open and available until he pulls you in (and you want to be pulled in). I think this should also be brought up by the man. Don't get mad that he's still online and/or meeting others, because you have not had that "conversation" yet. And if s/he is still online and talking to others, it's a good clue that s/he's just not ready to be exclusive. Or s/he is just not sure. You want someone who is emotionally available and is where you are in the process (or at least close to where you are).

Now, a good takeaway from the book, *It's Just a F***ing Date,* is a great way to present this is as follows:

Man: I just want you to know that I don't want to see anyone else. I only want to see you, so I'm going to close my profile. But, it's okay if you're not in the same place I am.

Woman: Really? Okay. Great (although this was shocking to the woman, but she liked it because it removed the pressure).

A few weeks later, she caught up to him and also went off line.

This is important to share because how often are two people in the exact same place at the same time? Rarely. In fact, if one person is way ahead of the other emotionally, it'll sometimes scare the other away which may cause a break up. So I loved hearing this idea.

11. I just made my first profile online and I'm overwhelmed by the number of emails and winks I have. How do I manage it all?

When one goes online for the first time, it can be quite overwhelming (especially if your pictures are well done and you have a quality profile). It does take time to sift through it all. I'd say start with looking at the actual emails (as opposed to the winks/smiles). Put a time limit of about an hour per day to look through the emails and respond to the ones that look more interesting. The rest will be there tomorrow. One can only manage so many people at a time. You get to decide how many you can manage talking to at a time. Everyone has a different comfort level and amount of time to meet new people. Again, the others will be there tomorrow or as the current ones fade away. Over time, it won't be as overwhelming. Enjoy the ride of meeting new people and remember to keep your expectations low because most of them won't be "The One," but dating surely can be fun if you let it!

12. What if I'm not getting any responses online?

This is tough. Others are talking about how overwhelming it is to get "hundreds" of emails and winks and your inbox is empty. Your fears are confirmed; "I'm doomed to be single forever." Don't give up so easily. You probably just need to polish your profile (either ask a few good friends or hire a dating coach). The first thing you can do is examine your pictures. Your primary photo needs to be your best picture with your best smile (and other photo tips listed earlier in the book). Make sure you at least have four good pictures.

Next, make sure your entire profile is filled out with no grammatical mistakes. Look over all the other profile do's and don'ts. An experienced online dater or a dating coach can also help examine your communication/messages you're sending. Finally, maybe the site you're on is just not a good fit for you. Maybe also try another one. You totally can't take online dating personally. There are so many good people (you being one of them) and for whatever reason at this place and time, the cards are not falling in place. Stick with it and don't give up. Chin up buttercup. Stay positive. Live a full life (not having online dating being your only social life). S/he is out there and will love you for who you are. So while you wait, keep being fabulous.

13. *What are your thoughts about instant messaging and chat rooms?*

I don't like them. It makes you too available and looks like you have way too much time on your hands (actually if you spend hours in these rooms, you *do* have too much time on your hands). Conversations can progress quickly and go to places that one would not go in person. Use the email option to talk and after a few emails (and a phone call) have the meet. No one knows about chemistry or personality until you're face to face.

14. *How soon should I meet someone I'm talking to?*

Email long enough to know if both parties are interested in learning more. Again, see if s/he can write a complete sentence and doesn't sound fake (you'll get better at knowing the fakes over time). After a few emails, moving to a phone call is a good idea (to see if there is voice chemistry—yes, there is such a thing). This phone call should be short, like 20 minutes. I've had several phone conversations that were slow moving with no energy and I decided not to meet after talking. If talking on the phone is a struggle, it'll be harder in person. If you move to texting, that's okay, but don't get into marathon texting sessions. Use it as a "staying connected until we meet" mechanism or meeting details. After you meet and know you're going to move forward, texting can be a fun and flirty part of the courtship.

15. Is online dating really safe?

You must have common sense when dating online. That includes not giving out any personal information (address, where you work, etc). Only give your cell number to those you're going to meet (although you don't have to. You can communicate through the site because many have the dating site app on their phone). Giving your cell number enables the man to call you for a phone conversation before your meet. Go by your own comfort level with giving your cell number. Online dating is as safe as any other method for meeting strangers. (One of my clients got a prepaid phone and only used that for her online men to call).

16. How should I initiate conversation? I just don't know how to start.

The best way is to always pull something out of his/her profile and mention it in your message. It shows you took the time to read it and points out what you have in common. Whatever you do, don't just say, "Hi" or "How are you?" One could probably cut and pasted that and sent it to 100 people. If you just can't think of a thing, say something like, "I enjoyed reading your profile. Would you look at mine and let me know if there's any interest?" If there is no response, there's no interest. If there is, you'll hear back.

17. *Are online dating sites better than the free apps out there?* (i.e., Tinder)

That would be a matter of opinion. It depends on your purpose in dating. If your goal is being in a serious relationship that will end in marriage or long-term relationship, most take the time to fill out an entire dating profile and pay money for being on the site. If you want something more casual, looking for friendships, hook-ups, or are just new to dating (and don't want anything serious), then an app will suffice for your purpose. Some people do both. Many 20-30's only use the apps only. It's quick and easy and fits into their lifestyle better. Try them all and participate in the ones that feel like a right fit for you.

18. *I've heard that Tinder is a "hook-up" app. Is that true?*

Tinder does have the reputation of being a hook-up app. You'll find players, marrieds, people looking for a threesome and people wanting a forever love. Can you also find these with the online dating sites? You can. I look at Tinder (and other apps like this) as yet another way to meet people you would not otherwise meet. The men (and women) who want sex only will very quickly let you know through messaging each other, that that's what they're looking for. Here is a conversation one client had as an example of such a conversation:

Chuck... Hi. How do you like this app?

Helen... This actually is my least favorite app. I only open occasionally on here. I have better luck on _____ site. I see that you are 42 and I am 50. Am I out of your age range?

Chuck... I always date older women. How long have you been single? Three years for me. My daughters are 19. I'm Chuck.

Helen... Good to know. That is rare (but, I'm glad). Most men like younger women. Why do you like older? More mature? I have been divorced for 10 years and have dated for 6. I'm Helen.

Chuck... What do you do for work? I am in radiology.

Helen... I guess you did not read my profile... LOL... I am a teacher's assistant and work at Macy's in the summers.

Chuck... Do you have any tats? If so, where? I have two.

Helen... No tattoos or piercings. I do have high values and morals. I start every relationship with friendship. Building a firm foundation first. (** The reason Helen said this is because she sensed it was getting personal quickly.)

Chuck... Are you very sexual? (** Hello?!?!? Good guess Helen).

Helen... Sex is great and fun, but I only go there in a committed relationship. You may want to mark me off your list if you go there quickly or recreationally.

Chuck... Do you like a man being dominant in the bedroom? (** Does it look like this is a high-quality man worth meeting for a lasting relationship or does he want sex only?)

Helen... That is definitely not a question I would answer if I don't know you. I am pretty sure we are not going to be a match. I'm sorry. Best of luck to you.

So, see? That conversation all happened in about three minutes. He quickly got to his purpose and Helen knew their dating goals were different and moved on. The next man she talked to she met. Even though they were not a match, he was a nice, new friend. So proceed with caution and definitely message a bit before meeting. If it's going to be a sex only person, s/he will let that be known (usually) fairly quickly.

19. *Should I join more than one dating service?*

If you're serious about getting out there and meeting people, yes. Join as many as you're able to handle (that might only be two). Yes, some of the profiles will be the same because many date on several sites at a time, but you'll also see a different crop of people (that only date on that site). If you only join one site, I'd suggest it be a large site where there are a lot of options and choices.

20. *What if s/he starts talking about sex before we even meet?*

Don't go there (unless, again, you're looking for a sex-only relationship). Most reading this want to become better at dating the most successful way. This is not a successful way to make a relationship last. If s/he gets sexual, just say, "That's not something I talk about until I know someone better." What about sexting? Same answer. Usually nothing good or lasting comes from sexting.

21. If I'm just dating, and not in relationship, is it okay to keep meeting different people?

Yes. In fact, remember that the one you're meeting tonight is talking to a handful of other people, too. This is a normal part of the courting phase. Many of my clients feel bad or guilty meeting/dating more than one at a time because others make judgments about that. As long as you're honest about where you are, and are true to who you are, then the person you're meeting will respect that. In fact, it's a challenge that might make the other like you more if you're not tied down yet. Meeting several at a time does not make you a "player." You're not having sex with them. You're just meeting and learning about different people. More about that in Chapter 13.

As I close this section, I'd like to share what Steve Harvey says. In his book, *Act Like a Lady, Think Like a Man* he said: "Newsflash: It's not the guy who determines whether you're a sports fish or a keeper—it's you. (Don't hate the player, hate the game.) When a man approaches you, you're the one with total control over the situation—whether he can talk to you, buy you a drink, dance with you, get your number, take you home, see you again, all of that. We certainly want these things from you; that's why we talked to you in the first place. But it's you who decides if you're going to give us any of the things we want, and how, exactly, we're going to get them. Where you stand in our eyes is dictated by your control over the situation. Every word you say, every move you make, every signal you give to a man will help him determine whether he should try to play you, be straight with you, or move on to the next woman to do a little more sport fishing."

The Meet-n-Greet --Moving from Online to In Person

The #1 thing I'm sure you've already heard is to always meet in a public place. Even if you've spoken on the phone and feel like s/he is safe, it's always best for the first meet to be in a public place. Exchanging cell numbers is fine (hopefully, you've talked or texted some anyway). Here are some pointers:

- Dress conservatively. Still accentuate the best part of you, but not too much skin. (I read somewhere you can show cleavage and your legs, but not both). Make your best judgment. If you dress like a commodity, you'll be treated like one.
- Men, if you're not sure what to wear, ask a female friend. Shave and wear light cologne.
- Always drive to and from the first meet-and-greet. Even if you've had "amazing" phone conversations. You still don't truly know this person! So drive there alone and leave there alone.
- Be on time. A little early is okay, but if you're going to be late, text or call to say so. Again, real life manners apply to all dating behaviors.
- Should I greet him/her with a handshake or a hug? Again, personal preference. That may depend on what type of communication you've had before

meeting. I'm a hugger, so I give hugs. But, a handshake is fine.

- If you're meeting for a drink, have only ONE drink ladies (TWO for men). You do not have to match what he drinks. The goal of the meet-n-greet is to see if there is any attraction and then make a second date.

- An appropriate amount of time for this first meet is one hour and no more than two.

- The best piece of advice I learned from the book *Was It Something I Said?* by Jess McCann was leave at the "Height of Interest." After about an hour of great conversation and you totally wish it could go on all night—THAT is the time to say you need to go. It'll leave him (and you) wanting more and then you can make a second date. More on that in Chapter 14.

- If you feel like the date went really well and you know you'd for sure like to see him/her again, I suggest you do this:
  - Ladies say this in person, "It was great meeting you. If you asked me out again, I'd say yes" or "This was such fun. I would go out with you again, if you asked." The man can choose to let her know right then he would like that or can say, "I'll text you and let you know." He can let her know later if he was feeling only friendship.
  - Men can say, "It was great meeting you. I'll text you tomorrow to see if you'd like to go out again sometime." The reason I like this is the woman

can either tell you right away, "Yes, I'd like to go out again." Or if not, it gives her time to figure out how to say, "No, I was feeling only friendship." It's not putting her on the spot right then if she's not attracted.

- If you or he asks for the "verdict" at the end of the meet ("Well, what do you think? Should we go out again?") You have two options. If you're brave enough to express your non-interest right then, go for it (just be kind). If not, a good standard answer is, "Let me think about it and I'll text you and let you know."

- Go with your *gut*. If something feels wrong or funny—listen to that! Don't dismiss it.

- Keep the conversation light hearted, asking questions about the other, but not too much like an interview. But, yes, it is sort of an interview. An interview to see if you like the things s/he has to say. Still no talk about sex! (Religion and politics are also still touchy subjects for a first meet).

- Most people know in the first five minutes if there is attraction or not, but give the meet ample time to talk. (Another reason I always say have a coffee or an after dinner drink). You can be kind no matter what. This might be the highlight of their day (or week) getting to meet the magnificent you!

- Here's a biggie for 35+ people. Because we all have a past of some sort, many singles feel the need to vomit *everything* on the first meet. (i.e. I've had cancer three times, had a hip replacement last year, my youngest son is in jail, I've been married three times and they all were a disaster, I cheated once the others cheated on me). You get my drift. Yes, all of that information should totally come out within the first three or four dates or so, but it's just too much for the very first meet. It's not lying. There is only so much information you can get out in an hour. A dear friend told me, "Well, I figure if I tell her everything on the first meet, she then can decide if she wants to see me again. At least I warned her about all the bad parts." Well, I can understand that way of thinking. We all want to be loved and accepted just the way we are and if someone likes us even after hearing the worst, then we feel like we've warned them. But, again, for most people, it's too much information too fast.

- You should not talk about your ex/divorce for the first few dates. If asked, maybe say, "I will tell you and don't have a problem talking about it, but I'd rather wait a few dates to explain because I really want to learn about you first." It's okay to tell how many times you've been married if over once. The older you get you'll find many, many have been married more than one time. You can speak with no shame because your story is your story and it will be told. But, on the first meet, keep it light hearted and stick to learning about your new friend.

One last comment about online dating. You'll hear from many that they hate online dating or that they had awful experiences. It's not the dating site's fault that you had a few bad dates. The site was only the avenue that helped you get the dates. So if you got dates and meets at all, that means you had "success" with online dating. It was only your meets/dates that were unsuccessful (which, like I said, if your mindset is to date and learn, you have probably had a successful experience. You just haven't met a keeper yet). You'll get better over time with screening out the bad apples. The best men I've dated have come from online and many others were great people (they just weren't great matches for me).

Reflection Questions:
If you haven't had successful meets, why do you think that is? (i.e. not screening well enough? Untruthful people?) If you've had successful meets, to what do you attribute your success?

What are some other specific questions you have about online dating that you at some point would like answered?

Chapter 4

SEX

"Men will not behave without standards."
-- Steve Harvey

THIS IS A HIGHLY PERSONAL and private issue. I would never presume to tell someone if or when it is a good time to have sex. This is definitely something that should be addressed when talking about dating because sex almost always is involved (not actually just the act of doing it, but the thought process with making the right decisions as it pertains to this). When I was in college, sex used to be a third date expectation/hope/aspiration. It is now, sadly, sometimes a well-worded text away. There are a lot of perspectives here. You can have sex on the night of the first date. An alarming one-third of singles do this! (One Match.com survey surveyed over half of singles do this—all ages!) Or you can wait until marriage (God's idea). Steve Harvey (comedian/author/talk show host) says don't give up the "cookies" for 90 days. Then there are a lot of options in between. There definitely needs to be a conversation about this, understanding each other's boundaries. If you're uncomfortable talking about this, perhaps you shouldn't be having sex in the first place?

Wendy Walsh says, "There's WAY too much free sex going on. We live in a high sexual economy." In her book, *The 30 Day Love Detox*, she reports a study of Mark Regnerus' work at the University of Texas. He found that people who have sex within 30 days of meeting have almost a 90% chance of breaking up in one year. Waiting 31-90 days gives you a one in four chance that you will be together in one year. There is no problem with waiting longer than that. The longer the better. Until marriage? Yes, even until marriage. Crazy idea, right? God knew what He was doing designing sex. In my observation in the single's world, I find this statistic to be true.

In fact, I think having sex too soon is the number one mistake why "next time" relationships don't work out (relationships at any age, for that matter). Men need time to get emotionally hooked and if women have sex too soon, men don't get emotionally hooked on you. Women *do* bond emotionally so much more quickly, especially after intimacy. Do you see the disconnect? So after having sex too soon, when the relationship doesn't last, the woman might say, "I don't understand. The sex was so great and he told me I was beautiful and he was crazy about me." Well, the sex *was* probably great but a man can get sex anywhere. Women are freely giving it away. Without building a firm foundation (and making that emotional bond), most relationships will just not last. I've observed this over and over again with "next" time around singles.

I personally think sex is the best thing God created, but He did intend if for marriage (I understand I'm taking a Christian perspective here, but just follow me). Since divorced singles already have been married and have already had sex, they seem to rationalize this and make it sound like sex now is no big deal. "We're adults. We've already been there, done that. Have had kids. I'm a 50 year old (insert your age) woman/man." So sex the second or third time around is different than the first time around. If you're a believer, is this what you think God would say? Would He say, "My child, I understand that you've already had sex with your first wife/husband; therefore, go ahead and have sex with multiple partners until you find the next one you'd like to marry. I was only talking about those teenagers and young adults who have never been married. You're different. It's okay for you." If not that, what do you hear Him saying? This is an issue we all struggle with—Christian or not. If you're not a Christian, I am guessing you still have values and standards and you want your next relationship to stick.

This idea came to me last night. In the beginning there was Adam and Eve. They were naked and not ashamed. God was at the center of their lives. God said, "Eat from any tree here but, whatever you do, not *this* one." Once they did, they knew they were naked and were ashamed. They hid from God.

Now relate this to sex for a minute. "Singles, you can date anyone you want, but whatever you do, don't have sex until you're one with me in marriage." Then what happens? When you do, you may be ashamed. We all know sex is a sacred, beautiful, wonderful gift God gave us. Not to just multiply the world, but to have pleasure and safety in marriage. We as singles love the pleasure part and forget the God part. Do we have grace? Of course! Are we forgiven (if asked)? Of course. But, the question is, after that grace and forgiveness, do we turn and change our ways or do we continue old habits ending up with the same results? Then we ask God why He hasn't brought us anyone yet? Maybe you're not close to God/Jesus right now. I mean you believe, but don't have an ongoing relationship with Him. I have many friends in that boat. Can that also change? Of course. He will never leave you and will help you through every struggle and circumstance. How do you do it? How do you get there? That could be another whole book, but I feel sure you know someone who has a strong relationship with Christ and that's probably a good place to start. Ask him/her to help guide you to a stronger relationship with Christ (or email me and I can help guide you). Now back to dating and sex.

It's true we become more comfortable with our sexuality as we get older. We tell ourselves that this is a need. This is not a need. It is very much a want. I am not just talking about men wanting it. Women are every bit as horny as men in middle age, so I am talking about both sides. If you choose to not wait until marriage, I think it's best to "go there" when you are in a committed relationship, have a firm foundation, have God at the center and you think you're going somewhere. Most just can't know that the one they're dating is "The One" in a few weeks or even months (even if you spend oodles of time together). Two people can then get past the lust stage, build a firm foundation in every other area of life first, before going there.

But everyone is different and has a different view. Actually, *most* singles the next time around have a different view. So I'd ask you, "How is it going for you with the way you date now?" You know the saying that if you continue doing what you have always done, you will continue to get what you've always gotten. If you have sex early (as amazing as it may have been), how long does that relationship last? I guarantee for most of you, it doesn't last longer than a year (and I predict a few months). You might be the outlier and have a story contradicting this. You may be the 10% to whom this doesn't apply. If so, I say awesome that you've made it stick. Truly. You are blessed. I have found that to be more rare. Look at your single friends. How many relationships have lasted after having sex too early? I think it's just something to reflect upon. Only with time and reflection do you arrive at a healthier place with dating.

Many people (mostly the men I have talked to, but definitely a few women, too) think this whole "waiting" thing is a bunch of bull! I would suggest testing it and see? See what happens if you build a firm foundation and wait on sex (I am saying twice as long as you have ever waited before) to see if your relationship lasts longer. Wouldn't it be great if you figured out that someone is not right for you *before* you have sex? It will save you some emotional hurt and disappointment (and another notch on your belt). Or try having sex soon and see how long it lasts?

Ultimately, you need to honor your values and who you are and do what you think is best for your circumstance. Like I said, divorced people are so good at rationalizing about this: "Oh, we've done it before. This is not our first rodeo. We are both adults here." If the other person caves in to that thinking, then boom! Another failed relationship. If you read *Cosmo*, *Glamour* and other magazines, you'll read articles saying it's okay to have sex on the first date or sooner rather than later. Many read those articles to validate their decisions so they don't feel as bad. But inside, they have scars. Wounds. Scar tissue upon scar tissue. Our culture tells you it is okay that we should test drive a car before driving. All your friends are doing it. It's been a while since you've had it and it's easy to get, so why not live it up? Again, just ask if your behavior is pleasing to God, if you are honoring the other person and his/her own values and how it makes you feel after another break up. It might be time to rethink this and try a new approach.

I know I keep saying this, but I think you'll find that it's *so* different the second time around. If your goal is to make your next relationship last, quote the statistic (above) from the University of Texas and explain to your partner that it's important for you to build a strong foundation first and save the physical until later. You get to decide how long is long enough for you (remember even go longer, if you can!) If the man is into you and thinks you are special, he *will* wait! If not, then maybe he is not a match for you. Maybe he just wanted to have a sex-only relationship with you or see how quickly he could go there before moving on? Just because there is physical attraction (that awesome thing God gave us) doesn't mean we have to act on every urge! Hopefully your parents taught you how to respect people and their boundaries (values). Hopefully you have respect for yourself that you don't give it to everyone (I'm talking to men *and* women). I think if two people have a great sexual attraction and they don't have sex, then that will just pull you closer together. If you want an everlasting relationship, one with a firm foundation that is based on everything else *but* sex, then waiting as long as you can is the wise thing to do.

Will you still have the *desire*? Yes! God wired us that way. None of this has to do with not *wanting* to have sex. God made it feel good for a reason, but just because there is sexual attraction doesn't mean you have to act on it right away or every time. Holding back for the goal of working out in the future is the intent. Having it be hard for both of you while honoring the desire to wait is a great thing. If you happen to have God at the center of your relationship, that is the ultimate. I also believe that if God (or your higher power) is at the center of your relationship, you have the chance of being more successful in relationship. So, if you want a greater chance of working out, most dating experts will tell you to wait as long as you can. There's way more to life than great sex. The older we get (especially if you are not going to have any more children) it's important to "like" your mate as much as you love him/her. If you look at the percentage of time you are in the bedroom and the percentage of time you "do life" together, it is a very small percent. An "important" percent, but a small percent. And what about the idea of actually being *in love* with someone before giving all of you away? Crazy idea, right? That's why it's called making love. Anything outside of love is just sex: the act of making love while not being in love.

Now, if both people are in that same space with wanting casual sex, and that is your value, then communicate that and maybe it will be right for you. I find that a lot of newly divorced people are not looking to find a forever partner right away so they just want to go sow their oats again and "live it up." If this is you, just communicate that you are looking for a sexual relationship and just be up front about it. You may find someone else is in the same place. (Beware of STDs! Because many are sleeping with many, STDs are running rampant! Middle-agers are not the highest population for STDs, but are the most rapidly growing age group for them). Again, this depends on your values and if this is something you think about nonchalantly. Some people never want to remarry, but want a long term relationship with someone. I would still suggest waiting as long as you can to build that firm foundation. Why add another man/women to your list if you don't have to?

Here's an excerpt from WebMD:

> Experts will agree that having an honest conversation with yourself about sex is just as important as discussing it with your partner.
>
> Cheryl McClary, PhD, JD, professor of women's health at University of North Carolina-Asheville said, "Every woman and man should know their boundaries before they start dating, and most of us don't."
>
> When McClary refers to boundaries, she's not talking just about the physical boundaries that come with sexual territory. She's also referring to emotional boundaries.
>
> "Emotional wholeness is crucial to the decision process of whether or not to have sex," McClary told WebMD.
>
> To that end, McClary often tells women, "If you value a committed relationship, ask yourself, 'What do I need to do to stay emotionally whole?'"
>
> When directing her advice on dating rules to a male audience, McClary puts

things a little differently. "Make sure your
brain, heart, and penis are in conjunction
-- they should all be in a straight line before
you have sex," she says.

Women, please don't believe that a man will dump you
if you do not have sex right away. Grown women think this
all the time (we will tell our teenage girls this, but won't
believe the same is true of us 35+ singles). In reality, men
want a quality woman and not one that'll sleep around with
everyone because she has the urge. If this *is* the case, is this
the type of man with whom you want to fall in love? The
one who will dump you because you won't have sex after the
third date? Or fifth date? Or sooner than you really know him
fully? One valuable lesson I remember vividly from the great
sermons series of Andy Stanley, *"The New Rules for Love,
Sex and Dating,"* is when he breaks down the love chapter
in the Bible (Corinthians 13:4). When the Bible says, "Love
is patient," that means one of you won't pressure the other....
ever! About anything. Including (but not only) sex! If one is
pressuring the other for sex, then that is not love.

You've heard that good things come to those who wait.
It's true! Men love a challenge and if you don't give it away
easily, it makes him want you more. This is true of any age
man! (age 16 or 66). Men, if you're the one driving waiting
on sex, it also makes the woman want you more. It goes both
ways. It's important to have your emotional feelings catch

Elizabeth B. Lewis

up to your physical feelings if/when you have that electric connection. Ask yourself, would I trust this person (that I've known for three dates) with the keys to my house, when I have to leave town, to feed my dog and water my plants? Probably not. What type of things do you think you should know about a person before giving all of you to him/her? Your siblings' names? Your middle name? Have you met his momma? Gone to her church? Do you know his life dreams? Future desires? You could make your own list. What do you think he should know about you before you give all of him/herself to you?

The sooner you do the "deed," the less you'll enjoy the process of the courtship. You just may skip the morning cup of coffee or walk on the beach because you'll hop to it a lot sooner. Don't skip out on all the wonders of discovering someone.

Some men might wonder, if she has sex with me so soon, maybe she has sex with others quickly. Of course, the woman might say, "I never move this quickly" or "I usually don't have sex so soon, but..." or "I've never done this before!" The truth is, if she "usually" doesn't do it this soon, then she wouldn't be doing it with you this soon. Do you want a high-quality woman who stands firm with her values and who she is, or one who just caves because you're hot and are saying all the right things? Okay, maybe not. But, I believe high-quality men that are looking for a forever relationship want to feel special to a woman, too, and not be just another number.

To back this up, here is what Steve Harvey said in his book, *Act Like a Lady, Think Like a Man.*

> Hold on, I know what you're thinking: You're thinking that if he doesn't get sex from you, he'll go and get it somewhere else, and you will have lost out on that one chance to get him to be your man—or he'll think you're playing games if you make him wait, and he'll move on to the next woman who's willing to take him into her bed.
>
> Wrong.
>
> [...] But guess what? He. Can. Wait. Yes, of course you run the risk of scaring him off, but isn't the guy who sleeps with you without any obligation to you, or consideration of your wants, needs and emotional well-being, the one you *want* to go away? Isn't reserving something that special for a man who earns it more of a benefit *to you*? You have the power to *make him wait*—to prove to you that he deserves your love and affection. The Power. [...] That decision is yours. We put our hands somewhere on your body other than your shoulder and you decide if we can keep touching that place or if we gotta let it go. Our job is to convince you to give it to us—to

allow us to touch it, let us have it. But the decision on whether we actually get to have it is Y.O.U.R.S.

Don't give up that power. Keep it. You only give up that power when the man has earned it, and he is going to respect it and do something with it. ...Your time is a form of payment.

Hugging? Payment.

Kissing? Payment.

You getting dressed up? Payment.

Going out with us? Payment.

Exchanging explicit e-mails? Payment.

But if he wants to sleep with you—make babies and/or have a family? Those are benefits.

In this section I have thrown a lot of biblical perspective your way. If you're still with me, what about those of you who are not believers or those of you who like hearing only facts from research? I just read *Love, Sex and Lasting Relationships* by Chip Ingram. He quoted five pieces of research that are not biblical. So, to be fair, I thought I'd throw this into the mix. He said,

Here are five significant facts about sexual purity that I have gleaned from published reports:

1. Those who abstain from sexual intercourse before marriage report the highest
levels of sexual satisfaction in marriage. In
fact, those who report they are very sexually
satisfied in their lives are not good looking
singles who have multiple partners and to
go barhopping to find the right person at
the right time for this exciting life. Research
done by Bethesda Research Group reported
in the *Washington Post* in 1994 concluded,
'Couples who strongly believe that sex
outside of marriage is wrong are a whopping
31% more satisfied in their sex lives.'

2. Those who cohabitate or live together
before marriage have a 50% higher pos-
sibility of divorce then those who do not.
Researchers at UCLA discovered that not
only do those who cohabitate have a higher
level of divorce, they are more likely to
commit adultery once they get married.
3. By contrast, the University of South Car-
olina in a study said that those who abstain
from sexual intercourse before marriage have
the highest rates of marital fidelity.

4. The introduction of sex in a dating relationship is almost always the ushering in of the breakup of that relationship. Doctors Les and Leslie Parrott made the statement after interviewing thousands of single people on college campuses.

5. Sexually transmitted diseases, including AIDS, can remain dormant, asymptomatic (you don't know you have it), for up to a decade or more, but be passed on to others during that time. The rampant spread of STDs flatly contradicts those who try to claim that sexual intercourse is a harmless recreational activity to be pursued with the largest number of partners possible. People are paying with their lives and their health for accepting that life.

Look, I'm aware that this is totally a private issue that is discussed between two people who are mature adults, but whatever your decision, there should at least be a conversation up front. Not the next day or a week later. It's too late. The woman may assume sex implies a commitment; the man may see it a variety of ways different than commitment. Remember that our brains are wired differently. If you are not on the same page, you can see how people get mixed messages and get hurt. I would definitely suggest *not* having sex with someone while profiles are still up online. Why would you give all of yourself away if the other is still "looking" around and/or is open and available and may be sleeping with others? If you're doing just fine with how you're dealing with sex in your relationship right now and you are happy, then hopefully this has just made you think about a few things. You have to do what you feel is right along with honoring your values and standards (as well as respecting your partner's values and standards).

Reflection Questions:

What do you think your mistakes in the past have been as they pertain to sex? How can you change that in the future so the next meet will be more successful?

_____
_____
_____
_____

What is the toughest thing about waiting? How long is a good time for you to wait? Do you think you could double that amount of time, especially if you knew it'd increase your chance of lasting longer in relationship and maybe making it as a forever couple?

_____
_____
_____
_____

Elizabeth B. Lewis

Friends with Benefits! (FWB)

Oh, how I hate that I'm having to put this in my book. This is a subject that those in the single's world already know about. If you're new to the dating world, you may be shocked to know this happens *all* the time. I could just not mention it and let you find out for yourself, but this book is about informing you what it is like the "next" time around. I was shocked to find out exactly how often it happens (and this is not it's just for second and third time arounders. This happens at ALL ages). As some evidence of this, data from the General Social Survey reveals that among college students surveyed between 1988 and 1996, 55.7% reported having had sex with a friend; among students surveyed from 2002 to 2010, that number jumped to 68.6% (Monto & Carey, 2013). If college kids only knew their 50-60 year old divorced parents, aunts and uncles were also doing this... ew!

I surveyed 167 singles (53.9 females and 46.1 males) ages 35-65 and 47.3% had a FWB relationship that lasted six months to two years. The majority of their first FWB happened when they were between the ages of 35-55. Approximately, 67.7% of the participants in this study said they had between two and six different FWB partners. When asked would you ever enter into a FWB situation again:

21.6% said heck yes. It was a great experience.

53.9% said maybe—depends on the person/situation/ where I am in my life.

86

24.6% said no for a variety of reasons, (i.e., I've had my fun and don't want to have this type of relationship again.)

(So 75.5 % said yes or maybe).

What is it exactly? Friends with Benefits (FWB) is a relationship in which people get to have sex (usually a lot of it) with someone they have no commitment to ("no strings" attached), without having to deal with expectations of being in a romantic partnership. There is more affection with FWB than with a one-night stand, but less than romantic love. Boundaries and rules are usually laid out before entering into this arrangement; for example:

- We can stay with this arrangement as long as neither is dating anyone. If one of us starts dating someone, the gig is up.
- We will only have this arrangement with each other and no other partners (because of STDs).
- No one can know we are doing this! Promise to tell no one?
- No "I love you" talk or emotional conversations. We are, after all, just friends.

Advantages:
- One who is lonely gets physical touch from someone s/he at least cares about as a friend.
- Physical needs are met (that one might be used to having in a committed relationship).

- For non-committal types this is a perfect arrangement. This is no commitment. You don't have to deal with "relationship issues." Leave your emotions at the door. Don't spend the night. You can have your cake and eat it too!

Disadvantages:
- You're second fiddle to whomever the other person eventually finds.
- Especially for women, it's hard to disconnect from that emotional bond you feel.
- You will eventually lower your desire to be intimate with someone who *is* special. It is not a special thing any more between two people who are trying to build something special.
- The arrangement is always temporary. Unfortunately, s/he may move on to another relationship (or maybe even another FWB because s/he still has to have that excitement of someone new. Hence, the problem when you find someone with whom you'd like to be committed).
- You will often feel empty over time because it is not ultimately what you want. Yeah, it feels good and it *is* a lot of fun (especially if you're having to sneak around to do it), but you're just using the other person for short term satisfaction (and being used).

- If your faith is strong, you will *really* battle with this because you *know* it's the wrong thing to do. You are giving in to worldly ways and not Godly ones. Your beliefs will convict you (and hopefully change your mind that it's not the best arrangement after all).

- Almost always one likes/has feelings for the other that are stronger than the other. The lack of reciprocity can hurt and be destructive. Rarely do these type of relationships turn in to ever-lasting love (but yes they sometimes do! You may even have a story to contradict this, but I would bet the vast majority do not end up being together forever). There is always an outlier.

- More people contract STD's because everyone is sleeping with everyone (I'm speaking in generalities, not being literal). What they say about whomever you are sleeping with, you are also sleeping with everyone they have been with is true! Some STD's don't show themselves until years later! (One of your boundaries should be to always use condoms).

- You usually do not get bells and whistles with this (no dinners, outings, flowers). It's usually a "transaction" that doesn't involve spending the nights or long all night talks.

- Unless you're very emotionally mature, you will be hurt when it is over.

- You promise to keep it a secret, but the other may not be as loyal to the secret as you. Especially years after it has ended. Then your reputation is tarnished. (Back to Andy Stanley, "Are you who the one you're looking for is looking for?") Do you want to marry someone who has these types of relationships with many and are you good with telling this as part of your story? It's just something to think about. As I always told my kids, "Every behavior has a consequence." Make sure you don't come down with an 18-year case of parenthood! (Wendy Walsh's warning)
- Remember how this will end. Do not go there with a friend you would like to have as a forever friend. It usually will not end well.
- FWB have more lifetime sexual partners than those who don't have these types or relationships. Again, think with the end in mind.
- Jealousy usually happens if/when the other starts seeing someone else. Again, this won't work if two people are in two different places emotionally.
- I've had a few friends break up; yet still care for each other and continue with the sex part of the relationship. They love each other, but know in the end that they are not going to be a fit. Their words say, "You can go date others." Their heart says, "Maybe over time we really will work out." Of course, two things happen here. One, it's hard to move on when you have this type of arrangement and two, when one does move on, the other will have a new level of hurt.

Some of this may have sounded judgmental (and maybe too "religiousy"), but even if you're not a Christian, your gut will tell you if this falls on the right thing to do side or wrong thing to do. You know the right answer for you and how you want your story to be told (we're all writing our own stories and whatever happens to us and how we respond is part of that story). The good. The bad. And the FWB.

One last thought: Another word/term for FWB is *uck Buddy. Not only is the F-word my least favorite word, but, would that be something you'd want on your resume? Do you want to be thought of in this way? As I told my kids (in one of our many sex talks) F***ing is the worst way to describe the most beautiful thing God designed and intended for a loving marriage.

Pornography

How I also hate to have to write about this, but it's such an epidemic in America, that I thought I'd share some alarming statistics. In my bibliography I have other sites you might want to look at. You could google and read all day long on this and just be alarmed as can be. I found this to cover a lot of statistics so I'm quoting from this site: http://www.fightthenewdrug.org/oneo-porn-stats-that-will-blow-your-mind/ This was written in March, 2015.

10 PORN STATS THAT WILL BLOW YOUR MIND

Porn has largely become mainstream in our society. From porn sites putting up billboards in New York City's Times Square to online news sources like BuzzFeed normalizing porn with seemingly every article they post, our society is having porn thrown in our face every day.

There is no better place to go than the online thought collector known as Twitter when looking for the popular opinion on any given subject. Tweets from hundreds of millions of users worldwide make it just one big massive reflection of our society.

So let's shed some light on it.

We're here to drop some truth bombs on you about the reality of porn.

10 PORN INDUSTRY STATS THAT NEED TO CHANGE:

(1) Porn sites receive more regular traffic than Netflix, Amazon, & Twitter combined. (HuffPost)
(2) 35% of all internet downloads are porn-related. (WebRoot)

(3) 34% of internet users have been exposed to unwanted porn via ads, pop-ups, etc. (WebRoot)

(4) Porn increased marital infidelity by 300%. (WebRoot)

(5) 30% of all data transferred across the internet is porn-related. (HuffPost)

(6) The most common female role in porn is women in their 20's portraying teenagers. (Jon Millward. *In 2013, Millward conducted the largest personal research study on the Porn Industry in the U.S. He interviewed 10,000 porn stars about various aspects of the business.*)

(7) Child porn is one of the fastest growing online businesses. (IWF)

(8) 624,000 child porn traders have been discovered online in the U.S. (Innocent Justice)

(9) Approximately 55% of teen girls living on the streets have engaged in prostitution. (Enough.org)

(10) Child porn is a $3 billion industry. (TopTenReviews)

Not cool.

Seriously, if this doesn't wake people up, what will? These problems aren't going away as long as people continue to justify the consumption of porn. Once upon a time, porn wasn't so common. It wasn't an issue that affected millions of people, much less an entire society. It wasn't a topic that needed to be discussed."

Noah Brand (author of *The Good Men Project*) said, "The problem is, learning about sex from porn is like learning about firearms from action movies."

Porn gives such a false sense of what God designed (to be a beautiful shared experience in marriage) and when teens and young adults watch this, they have many misconceptions about what intimacy is like. I could go on all day about the alarming statistics, and the only reason I'm adding this in my book is because if you're dating someone who watches a lot of porn, there may be intimacy issues in your future. A real woman's body will not look like that and will never be enough for a man who watches a lot of porn. And most of us are parents and it's important to be informed about how many teens are watching and getting wrong ideas (they, too, will be in relationship one day and better to correct and give guidance as boys than to fix them later when they are men in relationship).

Chapter 5

CUT THE NEGATIVITY AND COMMON MYTHS

FIRST, CUT THE NEGATIVITY! IF you are in the singles world for any length of time, you will hear a lot of negative things said. For example:

"Where are all the good guys?"

"Online dating sucks. Everyone lies."

"I guess I will just be single all of my life."

"I can't find a good woman/man."

"I give up!"

"I'm going to die a lonely man in a mental hospital."

If you are putting that kind of negative energy into the world, you are more than likely getting nothing but negative energy back. If you are not familiar with the "Law of Attraction," that would be a great thing to learn about. It's considered "new age" thinking and there might be parts you don't agree with. That's okay! Just take the parts that resonate with you and learn from them and apply to where you are. Especially the part about if you put positive energy into the universe, you'll get positive back. What you think about will come about. Negative begets negative. Fill your brain with positive thoughts like, "I am beautiful/handsome, worthy enough, a true catch." Not only does that feel better, but you will also attract positive people your way (some of those positive people being dates).

From whom do you seek advice? Other disgruntled single people that have had bad dating experiences? They will sit for hours and tell you their horror stories of their dates. Does this move you forward? Does this make you want to get out there and date? More than likely you will spiral down in a dark, no good feeling and negative place. In fact, it probably scares you more about dating. These are probably not the type of friends you should be hanging around with often. These same friends will be jealous when you do get a date or are happily dating.

Here are a few myths I would like to dispel...

1. *"You are too picky. You are never going to find a man/ woman to meet your too-high standards."*

Really? Does this mean you have to settle for someone who is not everything you want him/her to be? (I'm not talking about a perfect person, but rather a good fit for you and where you are in life). Remember, you are going to spend the rest of your life with this person. So settling for a warm body is just not an option. Remain picky/selective/whatever you like to call it. You more than likely know best what you need in a partner. No one else can decide this for you. And if you can't speak what it is, you'll certainly know when you meet him/her. The above statement makes singles feel bad. Having high standards is a good thing. Not a bad thing. People with standards have confidence and know where to draw the line. Keep your standards high. Embrace your singleness until you meet a good match for you.

2. "*Stop searching so hard. Love will find you when you least expect it.*"

Is this the same mentality you'd use in work and rearing children? Just stop being proactive with your kids and career and they will turn out just fine. If you're in sales, how about thinking that the sales are just going to come to you? Just sit back and don't try so hard. You'll get those sales when you least expect them. Little effort equals little results.

I believe you need to stay open and available in all the ways you're comfortable. Smile. Be a joy to be around. It is okay to look at the ring finger of the opposite sex when you walk in the grocery store. It does not mean you are going to go over and tackle him/her for a date. With your busy life, it is okay to be online and out there and available to be searched. God wired us for relationship. Just because you are looking for someone does not mean it is a bad thing. That desire was put inside us, so search all you want as long as you don't ignore your other life responsibilities (and the people in it).

But, remain open with a mental attitude of abundance and not scarcity.

3. *"You should keep him. There are not many good guys out there. At least you have someone."*

This comes from a scarcity mindset. This is what makes for bad relationships (and future divorces). If the relationship is not giving you all the key components you need in relationship for forever happiness, it is time to move on so you can be open and available for the one who is right for you. It is true that every relationship is not going to be 100% perfect, but you definitely need to have all the key ingredients, feel that it is the right relationship and you are still happy to be together. Remember the person who falls in love with you is going to love you for all the right reasons. The key question here is, "Does this person make me happy and make me a better person? Do we have common values and future desires?"

4. *"Only creeps and desperate people date online."*

This is absolutely not true. I have dated online for years and I am not a creep and am nowhere near desperate. People who say that have either had a bad experience with online dating or are judging by the horror stories they have heard. The nicest men I've dated have come from online. When one is a busy parent, professional, busy doing life, it is a great way to be introduced to new people traveling your same path. The alternatives are church, blind dates from co-workers or friends and bars. Some churches have singles groups, but most don't last for long. I'm guessing there are even more horror stories with blind dates. We all know what happens if you pick someone up in a bar- usually not the caliber of person you are hoping for forever love. That does not mean nice people don't go to bars. That means if you go for the purpose of meeting your next husband or wife, you will more than likely be picking up a barfly and/or a one-night stand.

5. "*She is out of your league. Don't even try.*"

More than likely, the person saying this is also attracted to her. Or he is jealous thinking you might actually score a date with her. If you are attracted, strike up a conversation. The worst thing that can happen is she could say no. And since she is already not going out with you then there is no rejection. Let me say that again. She currently isn't going out with you so after you ask her out and if she says no, she's still not going out with you. The only good thing that could happen is she could say yes! You truly have nothing to lose (except earn a new jealous friend).

6. "*Something must be wrong with him. He has been single for ten years and still hasn't found anyone.*"

Elizabeth B. Lewis

This is yet another negative judgment. There are *so* many factors that go into finding the right person. Remember dating is 90% timing, and 99% of those dates don't work out! There are so many reasons why someone may not be your match. Should you just give up? Of course not! Dating is about learning. The more you date, the more you learn. You learn what you like and don't like; need and don't need. If you are a high-quality man or woman, it is hard to find another high-quality person to date. I have many high-quality women friends. The high-quality men don't avail themselves every day (but they are everywhere). That is why remaining open and available is important. Stay the course, keep connecting, keep going on dates and meeting new people, keep working on you, pray, find ways to serve others, keep your active, enriching and fun life. God is still refining you and your future mate (and refining you, too). It is going to be more than amazing when it happens. You will say it was definitely worth the wait.

7. *"I'm just going to wait for God to bring me someone."*

Like Henry Cloud says, "Really? Do you have to do anything? I mean, do you have to walk outside? Or will he just be delivered to your doorstep?" I don't believe God will deliver him/her to your doorstep. Because of free will, we get to decide with whom we are in relationship. Nowhere in the Bible does it say He'll deliver him/her to us. God gives us options every day. I believe we have to do our part of being open and available so we can see the options that are put in front of us. Online dating is just one way. The others are listed in Chapter 2. Is it okay to pray for God to bring us our future partner? Of course. Any conversation with God is good and even though He knows our hearts, it's okay to remain in conversation with God about this very important desire.

"For I know the plans I have for you," declares the Lord, "plans to prosper you and not to harm you, plans to give you hope and a future." (Jeremiah 29:11)

Also Matthew 7:7-11 says, "Ask and it will be given to you; seek and you will find; knock and the door will be opened to you. For everyone who asks receives; he who seeks finds; and to him who knocks, the door will be opened. Which of you, if his son asks for bread, will give him a stone? Or if he asks for a fish, will give him a snake? If you, then, though you are evil, know how to give good gifts to your children, how much more will your Father in heaven give good gifts to those who ask him!"

I was reading The Faith Dare by Debbie Alsdorf and I like the way this was presented. She said, "I had asked, sought, and knocked... for months. Every time I got frustrated I was led back to the fact that it was good that I was asking, seeking and knocking on God's door! God has something good for my child and will answer my prayers on his behalf. [...] I'm still waiting, still seeking, still knocking. But, now I am also praising. Why? Because even though I don't see the answer today, I know it's coming. It's coming in the form of God's good and perfect will. God will give my child bread, not a snake or a stone... and in this I rejoice!"

8. *Opposites Attract!*

At first, when strong attraction is there, we talk ourselves into thinking opposites attract. But, over time, this is not true. Christian Carter says, "Opposites Attract and then Attack." It is more the norm to have common future desires, values, ethics, cultural backgrounds, similar financial habits and similar religion. In the end the opposite things will drive you apart and the common interests will drive you closer.

Reflection Questions:
Have you been guilty of saying negative things about other singles and their dating? Have you been the one being "gossiped" about? How does that make you feel? Have you believed in some of these myths? Can you find ways to re-think these?

<u>Reframing Negative Beliefs</u>

At the beginning of this chapter, I talked about all the negativity in the single's world. From comments others make, to singles bringing each other down with their bad experiences and horror stories. I now want to get a little more personal and talk to you about your own internal limiting belief system. This alone is getting in the way of so many singles and the way they think about dating. With every bad date or experience, people knock themselves down. Each time, singles think they are not worthy of love, not enough, and think they are doing everything wrong! Recognize that this is happening in your head and stop the madness.

Yes, it's good to reflect internally about what your part was in the relationship, as to why it went wrong. (Did you smother him with your need? Did you do all the pursuing? Did you not tend to her emotional needs?) We all have to take ownership as to why it didn't work out. Maybe you did nothing wrong and you just weren't a good forever fit. Perhaps you were being true to yourself by ending it. But when these break ups happen, you can't then have a belief of, "I chase men so I'm no good at dating," or "The way I date feels too desperate so I must be desperate," or "I'm never going to find anyone to love me." If you really examine this and are truthful, I suspect you can come up with many, many limiting beliefs about yourself. You'll then look for proof to reinforce that this is true.

"See? It happened again! I attract all the fixer-uppers and narcissists." After you keep knocking yourself down with what a bad person you are, you begin to believe this to be truth. It is not the truth!

Over time, you go into each new relationship with these limiting beliefs and they will prevent you from moving forward. The negativity leaks out. It's subconscious. It may show in your body language, what you say, or how you behave.

It's important to reframe these thoughts in your head. Good people tell themselves bad things all the time. I think it has become the American way. This leaves you empty and then you don't have much to give to someone else. So consciously reframe those beliefs. Flip it. Try filling your head with, "He and I were just not a good fit. We're both great people, just not a match," or "I know I need someone who can meet my emotional needs and he just wasn't able to do that. He's still a good man, just not what I need at this time." Tell yourself something different. What is the positive thing you know to be true about you? Tell yourself that!

Another thing I've witnessed by many singles in my single's group (Singles Meet Singles, or SMS).

Someone might say, "I'm not going to any more SMS events [or whatever group in which you're a member] because the men in the group are creepy and only after sex." (Really? Every one of them?) Or "I'm not going to any more events because there are too many people causing drama in the group." (Every one of them or just the few that you hang out with?)

That group [of singles or insert your own group] did not make the men or women act that way. It's his/her *own* human behavior that is making each act that way. They are going to do the same thing if they are part of that group or not. By saying you're not going anymore is preventing you from meeting the hundreds of kind and decent people that also may be there (especially if it's a large group like the SMS group in Louisville). That'd be like saying, "I'm not going to that church because Mr. Smith had an affair and I don't want to be a part of that church." Well, gosh, I'm pretty sure the church didn't make Mr. Smith act that way. I'm pretty sure he made that decision all by himself. He just happens to be a part of that congregation. My point is, don't let one bad egg (or a few bad eggs) keep you from connecting with so many others that can enhance your single life. Broad judgments (negative limiting beliefs) can make you believe your thoughts are truth. You're making it part of your manufactured truth, instead of the real truth.

Other examples of limiting beliefs:
- All men just want sex.
- Good men are hard to find.
- Good women are hard to keep happy.
- Men can't commit.
- Women are high maintenance.
- I'll never love again.

- I give up.
- Dating sucks and it's not worth it.
- Online dating sucks.

All of these come from a scarcity mindset (or from fear or a few bad experiences). We all have fears to work through and overcome. We all have shame with some of the past decisions we've made. Brene Brown, in *The Gifts of Imperfection*, teaches us that shame hates to have words wrapped around it. So that's why it's a good idea to go to therapy or hire a coach to help you move forward. You're a good person who has made a few bad decisions and there is someone out there for you. You're worthy of love and have a lot of it to give (to the right person) and you're ready to receive love. Until you find that person, remain open, available and positive! Reframe all negative thoughts and learn from all experiences.

Reflection Question:
Have you had a limiting belief? If so, write down that belief and reframe it.

Chapter 6

THE FIVE STAGES OF DATING

"In the beginning it's best to have less history and more mystery."
– Dr. Drew.

JUST LIKE EVERYTHING ELSE IN life, dating has a process and stages that most travel. Here are the Five Stages of Dating.

1. The Spark (Approximately 1-3 weeks)

This almost speaks for itself. It's that feeling we have when we're attracted to someone's "look" or "presence" or "mind." It's often called chemistry, which is that intangible feeling of wanting to be with someone more. There usually has to be some type of attraction to want to move forward or see someone again. Remember, the older we get, our pool gets smaller so if by chance you don't have sparks flying across the table on your first meet, yet they are a *kind* person, maybe think about giving them another date? Kind people are hard to come by these days so maybe explore him/her a little more.

Of course, if there is absolutely nothing, conversation doesn't come easily and your personalities repel rather than attract, you know this person will not be a match.

Common Questions

- *What if I was feeling chemistry and the other person wasn't?*

Well, you just can't manufacture feelings. It's either there or it's not. You can't take it personally because we all have our preferences. So if she says he was not feeling it, just accept it and move on. There's no way you can "talk someone into" feeling something that's not there.

- *When I see a cute man or a pretty woman (let's say at a party, bar or at the grocery store), I clam up and don't know what to say. What do I do?*

Think of the initial approach in terms of an "ice breaker." (More examples in Chapter 1). You're just making conversation to break the ice ("Great tie! You have a great smile. Did you catch the score of the game before the commercial?") If the other person also feels the same "spark" s/he will start making conversation with you. S/he just needs an opening. And if you're not interested and you know s/he are just trying to make conversation, you can still be kind. How do you know that his best buddy (who is currently in the bathroom or talking with another friend) won't be a person of interest? It takes courage to randomly talk to strangers (especially pretty or handsome ones) so just respond in kind. It doesn't mean you have to accept a date with him/her. This is how you make new friends.

Other tips for after the SPARK (remember these tips are all in the spark stage. The very beginning of dating someone new).

- Ladies, let the man pursue. After the first meet or date, it's best if you let the man initiate the thank you or nice to meet you. Men, in this day and age, don't wait three days to call or text her. Text or email or call (however you prefer to communicate) in the first 24 hours to either say I felt friendship or I'd like to see you again. If he doesn't send a message in about 24 hours, it's okay for women to send *one* thank you (although you should have already thanked him in person) and give an indication that you're interested – or not (for example, I totally enjoyed my time with you. Would love to learn more about you). This tells him you are interested. Then say nothing else. He'll pursue if he's interested (again, I'd wait for him to initiate after the first meet). If you give him a short answer to his initial pursuit (Thanks.) or (Nice to meet you, too). You're not giving him much to go by. If you're not interested, it's best to give the "I felt friendship" type response (given in Chapter 7).

Elizabeth B. Lewis

- When he texts or emails you, match what he gives you. If he asks you a question, don't give a five paragraph response. If he gives you three sentences, give him back two to four sentences (again, this is early dating while the sparks are flying). This is not game playing. It's strategy.
- Don't respond immediately. At least count to 100 or wait 15-20 minutes. This is easier said than done. You have your phone right in your hand because you're so hoping to hear from him, but you appear too eager if you jump right on every text and this sometimes comes off as too needy. You need to remain a little mysterious.
- One of the best pieces of advice given by Bobbi Palmer (The Dating Over 40 Coach) is "Discover, Don't Decide." This means instead of figuring out in a few days or a week that this person is not going to be a good fit for you (because of a weird quirk, or because he has a funny laugh, or she is really not as fit as you had hoped) just enjoy your time with him/her. I'll explain more about this in Chapter 8. Give it a few dates to see if this person can grow on you. You'll know in less than a month if this is someone with whom you want to invest more time—or not.
- Don't over-analyze (this is also easier said than done—I, personally, am awful with this). As you know, a lot of meaning can get lost while texting, so don't ever

talk about anything serious over text (I know most of you know this but, how often does it still happen? Maybe make a deal with your gal/guy to help keep each other accountable for this?) Otherwise, you may think, "What did he mean by that?" or you hear a tone that is not really there. Save the best conversations for face to face or the phone.

- Don't drop all your plans for him/her. Keep your full life, your friends and outings. Make dates when you're open and available. There will be time for dates.

- If he likes you, he will text, call, compliment you, be sweet, communicate with you and ask you on dates.

- What if he's not into you? (This can happen after the initial attraction/spark/great date.) He sometimes changes his mind about you for whatever reason. He won't text as quickly or often, texts will be short, might text when he's drunk or late at night (this means he wants a booty call--don't respond), won't ask you out as often and you won't feel like a priority. Don't treat someone like a priority that treats you like an option. This is why ladies need to let the men pursue. If they drop off the pursuit, you need to fall off of responding. And don't send the "What's wrong?" text. This will really push him back. Hopefully he'll tell you, but if not, just take his lack of response as "I'm not interested" (anymore). More on this in Chapter 13 when I talk about the push-pull.

- During the SPARK stage, things can be touch and go. You're in unknown territory. You have no idea what type of relationship he's coming out of. If she's meeting others, she might be trying to decide which one she likes the best. You don't know how she prefers to communicate. There are still a lot of layers to unpeel. You can only know someone over time! "Time will expose you or promote you" (Jeff Olson, *The Slight Edge*).

- Usually during the SPARK stage, you have not had the "Let's be exclusive" talk yet (something else I think that should be initiated by the man). So keep your profile up online (if you're online). That doesn't mean you have to keep meeting others, but relationship expert Rori Ray says, "Yes. Keep meeting others—several others—until he pulls you in (and you want to be pulled in)." More about "Circular Dating" in Chapter 8 on Perspectives in Dating. So many relationships don't work out anyway so why put all your eggs in one basket?

- Another texting tip: don't get into long texting sessions. This gives a false sense of where you are in relationship. When you feel it getting lengthy it's best for you to say, "I have to get to the gym. Text me later?"

- Last texting tip (for men and women): don't overdo the texting/communication. Sometimes it can feel smothering early on. You'll eventually find your pattern if you move in to an exclusive relationship.

- To be fair, if you desire to remarry and know this person will not be a good fit for you, it's best to move on at this level because hopefully nothing physical has happened. You will not be as emotionally invested and it'll hurt a lot less. Of course if you're just not sure, you continue on. Or if you're both not marriage-minded, you'll figure out if you're in the same place with dating. The key is to be honest because the next time around, you don't want to waste his/her time with just "dating to date" if the other wants to "date to mate."

2. Date and Learn (Approximately 1-3 months)

- This is the stage after you've decided that you can handle the initial known quirks, you like how each other communicates, how s/he treats you. This is usually when two people decide they'd like to be exclusive, meaning not date anyone else to see if you all can be an ultimate match. Of course, you're still discovering because it takes a long time to unpeel the layers of that onion. Each date, you're still deciding if this person can fit into your life with all your perfect imperfections, with your children, with your immediate family, with your faith, intellectually in every aspect of your life. Here are some common characteristics of this stage:

- You spend a lot of time together talking. Discovering.
- You'll ask a lot of questions. More discovering. This is fun. Not only questions like what's your favorite _____, but "what if" type questions. What are you dreams? Your future desires? Is it all still matching up?
- Observing behaviors—do her actions reflect what her words say? Is he considerate and does he make you feel special? Is she real? He means what he says and says what he means.
- You continue learning about little quirks (because we all have them).
- Usually during this time, you know that you're going to do something on the weekend together, it's just a matter of what. You start making plans together and going to places as a couple. Things are still exciting.
- It's important to keep your full life. S/he was attracted to you because of the full life you had when you first met. And it's okay to not have everything in common. In fact, it's best to have similar and different interests.

- Continue to be you. Don't conform to his/her ways just in the hope s/he will like you more. After more time passes, the real you will come out anyway so why be someone different than you are? In the end, you'll lose.

- Always go with your gut. If something comes up that makes your skin crawl or something feels wrong, listen to that little voice. This may begin to come out at the end of this stage.

- It is a good idea to have a mentor, coach, best friend with whom to process your relationship. Someone you can bounce conversations off of and questions to ask out loud. Of course, it's up to you in the end, but sometimes if you're falling for someone, you're not going to see red flags, but, your coach/mentor/ friend might.

- Enjoy your time with this person. It's still early—still in the first few months. No talking about "forever" yet. That's too soon and too scary for many. You can talk about doing things in the future, but maybe future means next month, not in ten years.

- Wait as long as you can for physical intimacy! If sexual tension is building, that's what God gave us. That's a good thing. Recognize it. Enjoy it! Let it build! Be as strong as you can and help each other be strong. Can you imagine how wonderful it'll be if you're actually in love and moving forward with this person?

3. Deeper Dating (Approximately 3-6 months)

It's around this time that skeletons start coming out of the closet. Maybe one of you has been holding back something that you only feel comfortable sharing when you're in a deep relationship with someone. I think these "skeletons" should come out sooner, but during the "honeymoon period" of early dating, each seems to remain on his/her own best behavior. So this is a very important time in the relationship. Here are some common characteristics to this stage:

- You'll find out how you each argue. This is so important. Where before maybe you all just politely disagreed with each other, you're now going to observe how s/he really handles conflict. Does s/he yell? Use put downs? Need space before talking? Hold in feelings? Like to hash it out immediately? Make you feel bad? Fight fair? Then after your fight do you kiss and make up? Pray? Are you more distant or closer? After a good fight, you'll know how your future will be with handling conflicts and problem solving.
- It's probably safe to introduce kids (especially if older) after a few months of being exclusive. But, that's a

personal preference. I think it's good to see how s/he parents. To some, this can be a deal breaker.

- Because you'll be more familiar with each other, you'll be more vulnerable and open to going deeper with conversations and sharing. This will usually endear you to your boy/girlfriend and may make you fall in love with him/her.

- You'll learn and observe insecurities about each other. These also sometimes take a while to emerge.

- During this time, you will be pretty sure if you can live with everything about this person you're dating. Not always, of course. The more vulnerable you are, the better. But, depending on the others' past experiences, it might take longer to have these things emerge.

- Your activities might become more relaxed. Maybe you've quit planning dates. But it's important to keep going on dates—some spontaneous and some planned. Keep making each other a priority and make the other feel special.

4. Solid and Real (Approximately 6 months and more)

- Usually by now the initial infatuation has disappeared and you still have a deep care for one another. You're known as a couple. You're seen together.

Probably worship together if that's important to you. And if it's not, you've worked out the spiritual part of your relationship. Your family and friends are starting to blend and travel to things as a unit.

- Your routines (both together and independently) have a pattern. Your communication is consistent. You're enjoying life together as a couple. You're probably starting to think about a future with this person and perhaps having conversation about this.

- Usually you'll know if you're in love with this person by now and if you can see a future together. I've had many friends and clients that truly were in love, but knew they were not a good match for each other forever. This totally can happen. (For example: you've discovered that your girlfriend has a mental issue and even though you're in love with her, you know it would not be good for you or your children to have this person as part of your family forever. Or one person is an alcoholic and the other person likes to drink. They could be in love and not be a good match. Or two people who want different things in life. Maybe the man wants to travel the world and the woman has young children at home and wants to keep parenting as a priority. This is why I say dating is 90% timing).

- If you're not waiting until marriage for intimacy, hopefully you'll be "making love" and not just "hav-

ing sex." Hopefully you're both moving forward at
the same pace—with goodness, love and kindness.
* Again—keep going on dates!

5. Long Term Commitment (Approximately 1 year to forever)

*"Real love moves freely in both directions. Don't waste your
time on anything else."* – Cheryl Strayed, author of *Wild*

This is self-explanatory. It's the level of being together
either a very long time or forever. It should be easy to determine if your relationship is healthy or not. You've gone
through every season, know how he fights, have processed all
her idiosyncrasies. You accept and love everything (or a large
percentage of everything) about this person. We all have different levels of comfort with commitment. If you desire to get
married, you need to decide how long you're willing to wait
for that. Are you okay with how things are now? Don't pressure him for a ring or push her to say yes if s/he isn't ready.
This should be a natural next step when it's time. Only tip
here is make the engagement is special when it does happen.
In addition to her wedding day, this is a momentous occasion;
one about which she'll want to tell for years to come.

Many books and surveys will warn you about the dangers
about moving in together before marriage. I know, it's con-
venient. It'll save money and maybe test your compatibility

before marriage. For some who don't believe in marriage, this may be your reason.

When researching these statistics, here is one I found that I wanted to share: http://divorce.lovetoknow.com/Divorce_Statistics_and_Living_Together (one of many)

Couples aged 50 and older are living together in greater numbers than ever. According to Forbes.com, more than 1.8 million Americans in that age group are cohabiting. Older Americans may choose to live together instead of marrying to avoid taking a cut in their Social Security payments or the survivor's annuity they receive from a former spouse's employer. Concerns about their estate not passing to their children if they remarry can also play a part in the decision to live together.

According to statistics gathered by US Attorney Legal Services, it doesn't accomplish the goal that couples think that it will. A couple who does not live together prior to getting married has a 20 percent chance of being divorced within five years. If the couple has lived together beforehand, that number jumps to 49 percent.

People who decide to live together may do so with the expectation that it will help them determine whether they will have a successful marriage with their partner. Divorce statistics and living together show that this is not the case. People who decide to live with a partner may also be more likely to divorce if they are unhappy with the relationship after taking vows, since they may have less conservative views of marriage.

During the time the couple lives together, they know that the situation may not be permanent. They divide bills and property in terms of "yours" and "mine," but, don't necessarily have the notion that assets belong to both of them. Living together may be more stressful than being married, due to the lack of stability. Even if the couple ultimately decides to make their relationship legal, they may not have developed the foundation they need for a successful marriage.

Reflection Questions:
In which stage of dating are you most successful? Have you experienced each level of dating?

_____
_____
_____
_____

Have you lived with someone in the past? Did it work out? Would you rethink that in the future? Why or why not?

_____
_____
_____
_____

Chapter 7

WHAT TO SAY?

THIS IS THE PART OF dating that is tough, for some. There are all kinds of circumstances that we are just not sure what to say. So, here are a few scenarios that may help you:

1. What to say when I meet someone, but don't like him/her romantically?

(I gave a few of these in the previous chapter, but worth saying again). Always be kind and honest. Saying this on text or email is appropriate if face to face feels uncomfortable.

- "Thanks so much for the drink and appetizers. Unfortunately, I was only feeling friendship. Can we be friends?"
- "Thanks for the coffee and great conversation. I wasn't feeling the way I like to feel to go out again. Hoping we can still stay connected as friends?"
- "You're incredibly funny, but didn't feel romantic feelings. But, what a great friend you'd be. Please say

we can be friends? I'll let you know the next time my friends and I go out for drinks. I feel sure we'll laugh at all your jokes."

- "Even though I don't think we're a match, I'd love to add you to our single's group. We have all sorts of events and because you're so much fun I know we'd enjoy having you join us. May I add you?"

- "I've been feeling lately that you might want something more than friendship with me. I feel kind of awkward *not* saying anything, so I'm just going get it over with: I don't have those feelings for you. I wish I could. Okay, awkwardness over! What were you saying about the movie?"

- "I am such a goof ball at relationships that I don't want to try something different with you and then mess it up. Can we just be friends? Please say yes."

2. *What if I go out with a man (or woman) for one-three months and figure out that s/he's just not "The One?"*

Face-to-face is always best, but by phone if that's tough for you. After 2-3 months, it's bad form to break up over text.

- "I've so enjoyed dating you. I have had tons of fun, but I need to feel more before moving forward. I'm just not feeling what I need to feel to move on."

- "As you know, I'm searching for 'The One.' For whatever reason, I just don't feel like you're 'The One.'" (If you know the reason then state the reason). For example, we are on different pages spiritually, or we have different future desires, or I grew up with an abusive father and when your temper flares, it makes me very uncomfortable and I don't think we're going to be a match, etc.).

- "I was hoping our friendship would turn romantic, but I still feel friendship. I wish I could feel more, but I know I can't manufacture that. It would be deceitful to keep dating you when I feel this way."

- "When I'm with you I *really* like you. But, when we are not together, I don't feel like a priority. I've learned to not treat someone like a priority who treats me like an option. I don't want to feel like an option. So, because of that I think we should part ways, hoping of course we can still be friends."

- "You're a great guy and I'm a great girl, but, I think we just date differently and need different things. (Name those things if you know them). But, because we're still both great people I'd love to hang out occasionally. Why don't you meet us out at the movies next Tuesday? We are all going to watch ____."

- All the other answers simply need to be honest and real. It may sting a bit if one person is further along than the other, but, always best to be honest (yet kind).
- "Over the last month, I've realized that we are no longer moving in the same direction. I like you so much and we *have* grown a lot. However, I feel that at this time in my life, we could serve each other better as friends."

3. *What if a man (or woman) starts talking about sex or something inappropriate that I'm uncomfortable with?*

- "That's not something I share with someone I don't know very well."
- "That's not something I feel comfortable talking about with you."
- "I wait a while before getting intimate, and the longer we date, the more we can discuss that. But, it's way too early (for me) to talk about that yet."
- "I am not a prude — there is a time and place for this conversation — but before, during or right after a first date isn't the time for me."
- I just watched a Matthew Hussey video (dating coach) about what to do if a man sends me a "dick pic?" This is as good of a place as any to share this. If

he sends it early on, unsolicited, you delete and move on. He's obviously only interested in sex. One man when early dating, asked his lady friend, "What are you doing?" She said she just got out of the shower and was getting ready to go meet friends. He said, "Send me a picture." (And he didn't mean the kind with clothes on). Hussey's suggested answer for the lady was, "I think you have me confused with the future me that has been on many more dates with you." It shows your standards and tells him it's too early in the game to do that. But after dating a while, when you're in a committed relationship, you might be more playful in this way. It doesn't mean you *will* do that. It puts him off and lets him know you won't be "that girl" before you have a better foundation.

- One time a man I was dating texted and said, "I just got out of the shower. Do you want me to send you a picture?" I immediately said, "No! Please don't." The next text was a picture of a shower with the word ME on the wall behind the shower head. It made me laugh out loud and I was so relieved he didn't send me an inappropriate picture. I saved that picture and will send that if ever asked for an inappropriate picture.

4. How do I explain to a man that I want to wait a little while on sex?

- If you feel him coming on strong, it's an important conversation. Start with, "We are moving a little fast and I'd like to talk to you about how I feel about sex in a relationship."
- "I think sex is the greatest thing God created, but, I only go there if I'm in an exclusive relationship (and we're both offline), and I feel like we're going somewhere. I like to build a firm foundation with the man I date, so I'd prefer to build the intellectual, spiritual, emotional, etc. first, and then explore the physical. Who doesn't like the physical? I just have found that it's best to build a firm foundation first." (If he doesn't want to wait, then you know his main motive. If a man really likes you and wants it to work, he'll wait).
- Quote the 30-day statistic from Chapter 4 and say, "Because of this, I want us to work. So I want to take all the mistakes I've learned in past relationships and throw them into this one."
- I've gotten intimate too soon before and it hasn't worked out so I like to wait ____ days before going there." (Again, if he likes and respects you, he now knows how long he has to wait. He can choose to stay or go).

- If you're one to wait until marriage, I would not bring it up on the first date but wouldn't wait until the tenth date. You could say, "As you know my faith is very important to me and even though we've both been divorced before, I have decided I'd like to wait again until marriage because that's what I think God wants; therefore, that's what I want. I totally understand if this is not your value but, I can't change who I am. This is a strong value for me and I'm going to be firm with this decision. If you choose to wait and date me, I'm going to ask you to also be strong because it's not because I don't want to do this; I'm just doing what I think is the right thing. I can promise it'll be awesome and worth the wait!"

- "People just have sex too soon. I've been one of those who has gone there too soon before and that has left me single. So, I'm now dating differently. In order for this to last I'd like to wait ___ days. I understand if you need to move on. I just won't compromise this standard again."

- "I'm just not ready to go further right now. We have so much more to learn about each other. I hope you can be patient until I can catch up to where you are."

Reflection:

Sometimes it's hard to know what to say. I'm sure you have many that are good ones. As you come up with good come backs and responses, write them down and share with others.

Chapter 8

DIFFERENT PERSPECTIVES IN DATING

AFTER BEING IN THE SINGLE'S world for a while, you'll see there is no one right or wrong way to date. There's only the way that feels right to you. And over time, that perspective will change as you grow and learn as a single person. When I first started dating I thought, "What's the big deal? Dating is just meeting and talking to people, so how hard is that?" Well, that part is correct. It *is* about meeting and talking to new people, most of whom end up as friends. But, it's about the attitude (intent) in which there are many different ways to look at dating. So here are a few I've practiced and others have learned about.

"Date to Date; Not to Mate"

I learned this perspective from Henry Cloud (author, speaker, minister, coach). He claims dating is not only about marriage. He said you should go in to the date with no expectations. No list. No types. Just because you go on a date does not mean you're a couple. The purpose of the date is just to learn. In fact, he says go out *knowing* s/he is not going to be the one but, just have fun and learn. I personally think this perspective is best when you're getting your feet wet after a divorce, or after a long term relationship has ended and you need to get back out there.

What he means about going out without your "list" is... you know that list we all have? Whether it's in our mind or actually on paper. He said when you date to mate, you're on the date mentally checking or marking off the things on your list. "Nope, she's not ____" or "He doesn't sound very financially responsible," or "She's not nearly as fit as I hoped she'd be." Or whatever is on your list. When you Date to Date, you leave the list at home, knowing s/he won't be the one, so you just learn and enjoy.

Some other things Henry Cloud suggests you do is have a "Dating Accountability Team." This is a few women and men whom you know you'll never date. These are the people who will support you in your singleness; the ones you run back to report how the date went, those with whom you can process. This is a great idea. Maybe you'll meet with this group once a week? Every other week? Enough to provide good support for each other.

He says keep a dating log. Who did you meet? What went well, what went not so well? Over time you might see patterns that you would not otherwise see if you didn't write it down.

Lastly, he talks about the importance of having a full life. Not pretending to have one, but actually having one. Don't cancel your plans to go out with a date. Arrange your date around your plans. You'll read about this in several books I've reviewed for you in Chapter 14 and I find it to be so true. Many of my friends will cancel their plans with their girlfriends because they finally got asked out by the cute man they've been talking to, all to find out that they were not really a match anyway. Keep your plans with your family and friends and accept dates only when you're free! Men and women are both attracted to others that have a full life.

"Discover Don't Decide"

I mentioned this earlier, but wanted to go more in depth. "Discover Don't Decide" is a great way of looking at dating by Bobbi Palmer. She's the Dating Over 40 Coach. She was a guest on my radio show and this stood out as a great way of thinking about dating the second time around. So often we go into a date wanting to decide quickly if the person sitting across from us is going to be a match or not. We say to ourselves, "I'm not getting any younger so I'd rather just decide quickly if we are a good fit or not and if we are not, move on." Well, it takes a while to unpeel the onion so the discover part is the best part of dating. At the beginning of the date you might think, "Oh wow. I love that about him. I can tell he's special." Then two hours later he says something that makes you think, "Oh my. No way. That's a deal breaker." Discover over several dates if the things that "get on your nerves" are things that can be changed. Facial hair? That can be changed. Being fit? That can be changed. Height can't be changed. Usually a person's true core can't be changed (and don't think you can change it). So instead of categorizing him in to a "You're the one or not the one" slot, just discover who he is. See if he can enhance your already fabulous life. Bobbi said, "I know it's so hard to keep our expectations, hopes and dreams in check. But, please go into your early dates with the attitude of just getting to know him and how he might enhance your life. Take the pressure off of both you and just be open without the burden of having to come out of it with a thumbs up or down. Take off those glasses, put your expectations on hold, and you might actually DISCOVER who your date is before you DECIDE who he is. How refreshing (and relaxing) is that?"

While telling you about Bobbi's perspective, she also gives this great advice: *Self-talk: "I hope I like him."* This excerpt is from her website. This was the one thing she learned from her coach that changed her entire dating experience. Bobbi said,

> For years I lived in a perpetual state of disappointment and self-doubt. *Why aren't they picking me?!* Then I learned these magic words: I hope I like HIM.

> We usually approach meeting men with the "I hope he likes me" feeling. Then, anything short of getting a second date feels like a personal rejection

and failure. But, what if you start with whether he seems to be someone you like? Can you see the difference?

The focus then shifts to how you feel and what you want and need. You stop trying to read his mind – Does he like me? What did he mean by that? – to what really counts: how you feel being with him and if you are having a nice time.

You can find out more about Bobbi Palmer and her advice and coaching at http://www.datelikeagrownup.com.

"Circular Dating"

In a nutshell to explain Rori Ray's "Circular Dating," it's dating several men (at least three) all at the same time. You accept the date with the man who calls first, and do not shuffle times or even think about manipulating the schedule in order to get dates with the man you like best, or dates to the most fun places. Rori says don't put all your eggs in one basket. This helps you avoid putting all your time and energy into one man until he claims you, as well as keeps you from being too needy or clingy.

By taking the focus off any one man, you accomplish two things. First, when a man realizes that you haven't made him the center of your world, it keeps him motivated to court you and win you over.

If a man senses that you are utterly devoted to him before he has asked you for a commitment, it makes you actually appear less attractive to him. Men fall in love by giving to you, and he can't do this if you haven't created the space for him to do so.

The second reason you want to keep dating is that it changes your vibe and makes you even more attractive.

By focusing on yourself and doing the things that make you feel warm and romantic and wonderful inside, you become infinitely more desirable. This is what I call 'dating yourself.' It means you treat yourself to the things you love. You buy yourself things that make you feel beautiful.

Instead of feeling desperate, you feel free. Instead of feeling needy, you feel generous. Dating yourself and flirting with other men makes you feel strong inside. It makes you feel wanted and desirable. Most important, it makes you feel that you have choices about how to be fulfilled and happy.

Having the right kind of vibe is the key to finding the right man and inspiring his love and devotion. And, when you do have that relationship you've always wanted, continue to date yourself in order to keep the focus on what truly matters and inspire your man to appreciate you forever.

As you can imagine, there's controversy with this perspective so take from it the parts that serve you. For example, perhaps you practice this perspective when you first get back out there. Meeting and dating several until you decide which one you want to date or the one that pulls you in. She says date as many men as you have time for, all at the same time, until you feel you have what you want in order to become exclusive. This is a personal call based on your feelings, not on "strategy." For example, if you're feeling anger and resentment, feeling confusion or neglect or a lack of communication, if you were to feel yourself "wanting" more then he's giving, exclusivity would not be in your best interest. So again, take the parts that work for you and discard the rest.

To find out more about Rori Ray (who has all sorts of dating books, videos and programs) go to http://www.havetherelationshipyouwant.com

How to Attract Love Without Drowning in the Dating Pool

We read dating blogs and relationship books. We long for love. Spend hours scowling at profiles.

Bex Burton, heart trainer and life coach, said on her webcast, "Sometimes we need to think differently about love. Your blocks to divine love are within you, not beyond you." Here is what she prescribes.

1. Silence the Noise! This means deactivate all online dating accounts (for one month)
2. Be in the Spirit of Divine Love

- Law of Attraction—we may hear it over and over again, but we need reminders. We attract what we give our thoughts to. If you don't know about the "Law of Attraction," watch *The Secret* or google it (and there are plenty of books on the subject. Take the parts that speak to you and discard the rest.)
- Bex says when we search, we live in lack.

Actions we can take:

- Softness/forgiveness: Don't beat yourself up for not being in a relationship, or over your break up. Open awareness to inner critic. Say, "I am imperfect, but I am love."
- Witness: Witness divine love in other couples. Notice it, even with friendships being honest with each other. Family—look for signs and symbols of love (like a heart, love words, etc.) Say, "Love is Coming from Everywhere."
- Observe: Watch how people interact, especially in magnetic interactions; how they use touch.
- Absorb the feelings and interactions of others. Feel the love.
- Don't roll eyes at happy couples. Instead, delight/ relish/desire—When you see those happy couples, don't say, "Oh gross. Get a room." Say, "That is beautiful. I want that!"
- Write and Reflect: Make note of every instance you experience love in any way, every day, like when you

see someone opening a door, sweet text, billboards, people kissing, etc.

- Say, "Love is coming. You're near. I can feel you."
- Say often, "Love is on the way to find me!"

3. Share Your Abundant Love with the World.

- What big dream would you pursue if time and money were not an option?
- Tackle your big, ridiculous, divinely passionate dream.

What is stopping you? What story are you telling yourself that won't let you do this? To find out more about Bex Burton, go to BexBurton.DreamBuilderCoach.com.

"It's Just a Date"

The last perspective that I'll present is to think, "It's just a stinkin' date." (This idea is from the book It's Just a F***ing Date by Greg Behrendt and Amira Routola (I don't like the "F" word in the title, but it is chalk full of good dating advice and ways to look at things). Since most of the meets/dates you have are not going to work out, just say to yourself, "It's just a date." It's not a commitment. Not a marriage proposal. You don't even have to commit to a second date. But, go and enjoy yourself and learn. That's the beauty of dating. Remember, if you're not having fun, you probably should take a break and just work on you.

Reflection Question:

Which perspective resonates with you right NOW? You may find over time you'll change your perspective. That's totally okay. As we date and learn, we change our mind of what we think is best for us.

Chapter 9

RELATIONSHIPS AND FACEBOOK

FACEBOOK IS A GREAT TOOL, but can also be a detriment to many relationships. (This will relate to all social media, but we'll use Facebook as the example here). It's true that there are over 1.44 billion monthly active Facebook users (source: Facebook as of April 22, 2015). It's hard to get away. It seems like everyone is on Facebook (but we all know a select few that will not log in or come close to getting on Facebook). Even though we all have varying degrees to which we use social media, there are a few lessons I've learned and observed over the years. (I'll separate these lessons into three categories: friendships, dating relationships and marriages).

Friendships

How hard it is to not get sucked in to "Their life is better than mine?" With the pictures of other's trips, relationships, activities, it can make you feel like less or that you're not enough. If you *were* enough then why don't you get all the party invites and take all the trips? It's the equivalent to not getting invited to the all parties in high school, then having everyone talk about them Monday at school. The reality is everyone is fighting his/her own battle. We all have our own bits of loneliness, unhappiness, struggles, etc.

Another common phenomenon is FOMO (Fear of Missing Out). Some people don't want to miss a single event, happening, announcement. They always want to be in the know. So, just like any other activity in which we choose to participate, it's important to set boundaries. Telling yourself (and maybe set a timer) how long you're going to be on Facebook is a great idea. And the ones you really want to know about, you put in your "close friends" so you can start there. Read what your favorite people are posting over everyone else. Remind yourself that your life is pretty fabulous and having that life show on Facebook doesn't make it any more fabulous. Let go of all comparisons.

<u>Dating Relationships</u>
This is a tough one in so many ways. I'll try to hit some of the biggie issues.

- At what point are you a "real couple?" Some people say it's after you're Facebook official and declare "in relationship." The majority of relationships just don't last (have you noticed that?) So if you declare that, and then you break up, you have to go back to "single." Then *everyone* wants to know what happened. I'd suggest don't claim "in a relationship" ever. Go from single to engaged or single to married. If you're in relationship, all your family and friends will know it without Facebook nation having to know or affirm and comment.

- Now, what if you're dating and a woman starts talking to your boyfriend on Facebook? First, there's a simple "like" of a picture, then a comment and before you know it, private messaging. The pre-Facebook equivalent to this would be you're at a party and another woman says to your boyfriend, "Hey, come over here so we can talk privately away from all these people," (while your girlfriend is in the other room). In my opinion, it's up to the boyfriend to draw a boundary and say, "Hey, I'm dating someone and don't feel right talking to other females even if they are just friends. Maybe we will see you out and about soon?" The "other woman" (or man if reversed) should also not cross over that private message boundary. A good guideline is if you're writing a message you wouldn't mind your boy/girlfriend reading over your shoulder, it's probably okay. In fact, maybe even show it to your boy/girlfriend in the interest of full disclosure.

- It's important to remember this really isn't a Facebook problem, it's a human behavior problem. If your gut tells you it's the wrong thing to be doing, it is. Facebook is just the tool people are using to communicate and blur the lines.

- Jealousy means there is no trust. It's important to agree upon what and how much you and your boy/girlfriends want to post/tag/respond. It's an easy conversation and compromise.
- Facebook secrets are also not a good idea if you're in relationship. After all, being in relationship means you're trying to build something special that might even end in marriage. So full transparency will always be important. Don't try to secretly accept a friend request from an ex. If someone is all over your partner's wall and seems to show a level of intimacy and humor with him/her that you're not privy to, the fact that s/he has not talked about this person could be a sign that there's really something to hide.
- A common question I get is, "Should I delete all my old boy/girlfriend's pictures off Facebook? If so, how soon after?" My answer is when it feels right, do so. Some do it immediately because it was a bad break up or you're angry or it's a great way to get over the one who hurt you. If it was a nice break up and you ended as friends and you think, "Well this person was just part of my life and it brings me great memories," I'd say when you start dating someone else, it won't feel right to you to have the previous person on there after a while. Yes, that person was part of your past, but, if your gut tells you that it's not right to have so many posted for all your future boy/girlfriend's family and

friends to see, it isn't. Maybe save them to a memory stick to keep for old times' sake. Just take them off of Facebook. What if you flipped it around, would you like to see your boyfriend's old girlfriend's pictures on there? If not, then he probably won't want to see yours.

- Do not be misled: "Bad company corrupts good character." (1 Corinthians 15:33)

Marriages (I know this is a book about being single, but one day we want to be married again, so I'm including this. This will also apply to those who don't want to remarry, but want to forever be in a long-term relationship).

A lot of the same rules from the "dating" category above apply here: Transparency, no secrets, no private conversations your spouse can't see.

- You've heard of some married couples sharing a Facebook page. That is a great idea! Then no secrets or private conversations can be had. If you're not cool with that, then share passwords or have part of your evening be being on Facebook together- laughing and talking about your friends' posts. (Facebook *can* be quite entertaining).
- A few signs that your partner is Facebook-cheating:
  - S/he is often lost in thought within his/her texting conversations and never shares what s/he is discussing. Now we all have private conversa-

tions, but, if this happens frequently taking more time away from each other rather than being present with each other, then his/her attentions/priorities may be elsewhere.

- S/he gets texts at all hours of the day and even late night. I'm not talking about a child or a friend who really needs you at 11:00 p.m., but if online conversations regularly make their way in to your bedroom late at night, then again, you're second fiddle to that other relationship.

- S/he is physically possessive of his phone/iPad. Again, if you're trying to hide something, it's usually something you don't want your spouse/partner to see.

- He gets defensive about how much time he in on his phone. Why else would he get so riled up? When married or in a committed relationship, I say full rein on the other's phone is appropriate. When I'm in a committed relationship with someone, he has full rein of my phone. (I run a single's group, so it is very important for me to do that! He can look at my phone or Facebook at any time!)

- My favorite verse is 1 Corinthians 13: 4-7: "Love is patient and kind; love does not envy or boast; it is not arrogant or rude. It does not insist on its own way; it is not irritable or resentful; it does not rejoice at wrongdoing, but, rejoices with the truth. Love bears all things, believes all things, hopes all things, and endures all things." (Even on Facebook)

These relationships are not limited to relationships with pre-existing problems. Facebook presents so many challenges to committed relationships that Jason and Kelli Krafsky wrote a book called, *Facebook and Your Marriage.* It's a guide for married people who want to know the best ways to do Facebook and not put their marriage at risk. It's full of answers, tips, and insights for how to use Facebook, protect your marriage, enhance your relationship and deal with the many issues and situations that can come on the world's most popular online social network.

So, let Facebook be something fun you do together if you're in relationship. If you're not, don't think the whole world is having more fun than you. You are enough just the way you are. Everything in moderation. Seek balance. We still need to remember who we are and build each other up and not tear each other down! Use Facebook for the greater good and not bad.

"Now the works of the flesh are evident: sexual immorality, impurity, sensuality, idolatry, sorcery, enmity, strife, jealousy, fits of anger, rivalries, dissensions, divisions, envy, drunkenness, orgies, and things like these. I warn you, as I warned you before, that those who do such things will not inherit the kingdom of God. But, the fruit of the Spirit is love, joy, peace, patience, kindness, goodness, faithfulness, gentleness, self-control; against such things there is no law" (Galatians 5:19-26).

Reflection Question:

What issues have you had with Facebook and relationships? Talk to someone about the best way to proceed.

_____
_____
_____
_____

Chapter 10

HEALTHY RELATIONSHIPS

"We come to love not by finding a perfect person, but, by learning to see an imperfect person perfectly."
—Sam Keen

HEALTHY RELATIONSHIPS COME IN DIFFERENT shapes and forms, but many have common characteristics. If I asked you to name couples who have a healthy relationship, could you immediately name a few couples and tell why they are healthy? I bet some of the reasons would include mutual respect, support, good communication, compromise, kindness and maybe even a strong spiritual relationship. Some think healthy means crazy romantic, like in the movies. It may begin that way, but you'll eventually come to a more mature type of love. Healthy love involves two people being whole emotionally, and together mentally, working toward a common goal. An unhealthy relationship involves being mean, controlling, disrespectful and maybe even abusive. Below are some indicators that you may have a healthy relationship. (Pat yourself on the back if your relationship has these characteristics or strive to have these in your next relationship).

- Total acceptance of your partner's perfect imperfections. Snoring all night, passing gas in the morning, the way they deal with phone solicitors and bad waiters, etc. No one will be 100%, but being able to love your partner, despite his/her imperfections, is key.

- Being intentional about giving your partner what s/he needs. Thinking about his/her needs before your own. This is a tough one because unhealthy couples get stuck in the "What does this relationship do for me?" Instead of "What can I do for him/her?" which in turn feeds you. If you don't know about *The 5 Love Languages* (Gary Chapman), I highly recommend you read and learn about these. You can get the book or google and read about these (and take a test) online. It's important we learn what our partner's love language is and give to him/her how each receives love. Not give your partner how *you* receive love. That's what s/he learns and gives to you!

- I'm going to quote Andy Stanley again (my weekly class has participated in many of his studies). In *The New Rules for Love, Sex and Dating*, Andy breaks down the love chapter in the Bible (1 Corinthians 13). Here are some great takeaway points I like to remember, teach and apply.

- Love is patient, meaning you'll never pressure your partner— EVER. If there is pressure (about anything), that is not love.
- Love is kind, meaning considerate. Thinking about the other before yourself.
- Love does not envy, meaning not only being jealous, but, I don't feel too good about me, so I'm going to make sure you don't feel so good about you.
- Love does not boast, meaning don't try to always top his/her story. Let him/her bask in the glory of his/her story.
- Always a biggie is how you fight! Obviously, even healthy couples fight, but do they bring up past hurts and faults? Do they put the other down? Do they scream and yell? Or do they stick to the issue at present and try to resolve that issue, still speaking their mind, but not getting out of control with making the other feel bad about his/her opinion? Do they seek to understand his/her point of view, which sometimes helps resolve the issue? Remember if you're always kind, this won't be a problem. Which brings me to the next attribute.
- Compromise: there is no way we will always get our way. Healthy couples learn how to give a little and take a little. When you don't get your way, you have to let it go. Don't bring it back up later when it's to

your advantage. This is how couples start keeping score.

- No keeping score. Yes, sometimes you may do the majority of the house work or grocery shopping. S/he may bring home more of a salary and do the yard work, but if you keep score, then resentment sets in. Just know that sometimes you're going to have to carry more of the load and s/he will have his/her turn to carry the load. If it's all done out of love, it won't matter.

- No secrets: healthy couples share everything of importance with the other. It doesn't have to be what you ate at each meal or every conversation at work, but all things that matter are shared. This builds trust especially if confidences are kept.

- Very few issues with intimacy. Healthy couples know that being intimate is the ultimate expression of love.

When I was reading *Psychology Today*, I found an article by Alice Boyes, Ph.D called "50 Characteristics of Healthy Relationships." I liked these so I wanted to include them in my book. I found all of them valuable, but I'm including my favorites here. To read the whole list go to https://www.psychologytoday.com/blog/in-practice/201301/50-charac-teristics-healthy-relationships

If you can say yes to most of these, it's very likely you're in a healthy relationship:

1. You can name your partner's best friend and identify a positive quality that the person has.

2. You and your partner are playful with each other.

3. Even when you disagree, you can acknowledge your partner makes sensible points.

4. You see your partner as trustworthy.

5. Your partner is enthusiastic when something goes right for you.

6. You know your partner's aspirations in life.

7. You kiss every day.

8. You're comfortable telling your partner about things that make you feel vulnerable such as worries about getting laid off.

9. You have your own "love language" (pet names or special signs you give each other).

10. You never, or very rarely, express contempt for your partner by rolling your eyes, swearing at them, or calling them crazy.

11. You can list some positive personality qualities your partner inherited from their parents.

12. You have a sense of security: You're confident your partner wouldn't be unfaithful, or do something to jeopardize your combined financial security.

13. When you argue, you still have a sense that your partner cares about your feelings and opinions.

14. Your partner lets you into their inner emotional world—they make their thoughts and feelings accessible to you.
15. You frequently express appreciation for each other.
16. When you say goodbye in the morning, it's mindful and affectionate.
17. You don't flat-out refuse to talk about topics that are important to your partner.
18. You respect your partner's other relationships with family or friends, and view them as important.
19. You're physically affectionate with each other.
20. When you feel stressed or upset, you turn toward your partner for comfort, rather than turning away from your partner and trying to deal with it yourself.

Questions:

Have you seen couples who have healthy relationships? Who are they? What characteristics do you see in them that you'd like to have in your next relationship?

_____
_____
_____
_____

Chapter 11

The Break Up, Before and After

So, how do you know that you're just not going to work out? You may have dated this person anywhere from three months to a year and you're starting to wonder if this is a good forever match for you.

20 Possible Signs that You Might Need to Break Up

Here is a list of 20 possible signs that it might be time to break up. (If over half of these are you, breaking up might be something you might consider).

1. You continue having doubts in your head—a little of this may be normal, but, if these thoughts pop up often, don't ignore them.

2. You find yourself talking/asking your friends/family, "Do you think ___?" Whatever the question, you're asking for their opinion about what they think. You're looking for validation. If you were sure, you wouldn't care much what your family and friends think. If they come to you with concerns, it might be a good idea to at least listen?

3. If trust is lost, then jealousy will surely follow. Jealousy means there is a lack of trust. You can't be in relationship with someone with whom you have lost trust.

4. You disagree on big things (parenting, religion, caring for elderly parents).

5. You fight more often and sometimes fight unfair. How you fight as a couple is so important. There will not always be peace and harmony, but how you deal with conflict could very well drive you apart.

6. Your future desires are different. It's important to have similar desires or at least be supportive of your partner's future desires and be able to live with them.

7. If you've become intimate, one sign someone is moving away from you is that activity will happen less frequently. You'll know that they are not really "there" when you are intimate.

8. Future talk (which may have been there before) is no more.

9. The things you used to love to do as a couple, you'd now rather do alone.

10. If you used to share everything and now there are secrets, this may be a sign that one of you is pulling back.

11. If your partner is pressuring you to do something you don't want to do (sex, drinking, drugs, something

criminal) and then says, "If you loved me, you'd do it." That is not love. Time to move on.

12. Issues of which you were not aware (alcoholism, hidden drug issues, mental issues) emerge. Good to get out now instead of trying to be co-dependent.

13. Your partner becomes controlling and manipulative. This is not something that will improve over time. In fact, it will get worse over time. Time to fly.

14. If you try to get back and break up several times, these relationships almost always do not work out in the end. This is usually because you want it to work and there is so much good about this person. The reason you broke up in the beginning is probably not going to magically go away (unless therapy is involved and both parties are making a big effort to change it for the better).

15. You find that you don't miss him/her anymore when s/he is out of town or you're away from each other over a few days.

16. If lying and cheating are happening, these, too, don't quickly just go away. There is a reason someone lies or cheats. Something in the current relationship is not working.

17. "New and exciting" eventually go away. How are you two when bored together? If the silence and boredom become awkward and uncomfortable, this is a sign of not being compatible. A couple in love is

just as happy bored as they are doing something new and exciting. So if boredom is a problem, something else is wrong, but you may call it boredom.

18. If you find your partner is always trying to change you or you're trying to change him/her, this will not work out in the end. You need to accept each for who each is and be okay with it. Men and women are just different. We all have our flaws.

19. Some are just not going to be a forever match. Your dates have been fun. There have been lots of laughing and good times, but as a forever love, you can't see it. It's just as deceptive staying with someone you know will not be an ultimate match for you as it is to tell any other lie. But, be sure the reasons you're breaking up don't have to do with you and your expectations. Maybe it is just a case where someone is ahead of you emotionally and you need to catch up? Rarely do people fall in love at the same pace.

20. You find yourself being attracted to other women/men (beyond the normal "I think he's a handsome man" thought). You definitely don't want to cheat and thinking it's greener on the other side of the fence is a common mistake. The grass is greener where you water it. So water where you are and don't jump over the fence. But, if you find yourself climbing over the fence, break up first! Don't cheat!

A common question I get is, "Is it bad to break up on text or email or do I always have to do it in person?" My answer is two-fold. First, how would you like for someone to break up with you? The answer is not always in person. If you're a crier or one of you has a bad temper, you might prefer to not do it in person. Secondly, in person is usually best because both parties can get out any questions and there is closure. But I think it also depends on how long you've gone out. If you've dated less than a month and were casual, not intimate, a text and/or email is fine. If you've been exclusive for longer than a month, have been intimate or have dated a long time, in person is the most respectful way, with the phone being the next best acceptable way. Breaking up with someone with whom you've had a great relationship, deserves more than a text or an email.

Reflection Questions:
Have you experienced some of these before? Have you stayed too long in a relationship that you knew needed to end? What will you do differently the next time this happens?

_____
_____
_____
_____

After the Break Up
You may have thought that the actual breaking up with someone was the hard part. The harder part is actually get-

ting over your break up so you can move on. A good rule of thumb to totally get "over" someone is take one week for every month and one month for every year you were in relationship with no communication. (For example: If you date a man/ woman for 6 months, it'll take about 6 weeks to emotionally get over him/her – give or take a few weeks). Some say this is a myth because everyone is different with his/her feelings. That's generally true, so that's why I say this is a *general* rule of thumb. It might take way longer or way shorter.

The key to totally healing is *zero* communication with this person. Every text or conversation you *do* have (which may give you a ray of hope), means you have to set the clock back and start over with the time apart for healing. Why? Because the one with the most invested takes the longest to heal. Zero texting, emailing, stalking on Facebook/social media, following his/her routine hoping you'll "accidentally" run in to him/her, checking in with him through friends, etc. This is so hard. Your friends will come give you reports about seeing him out or telling you who he's asked out. Politely ask your friends to not give you any reports. This makes it hurt all the worse. You might say, "Do you mean if I was married 15 years, it'll take me 15 months to heal?" Yes (as a rule of thumb, not an absolute). Getting over a break up is like when you fall and cut your knee; you'll form a scab. Over time, that scab will heal and you'll grow new skin. Eventually it won't hurt any more at all. You may have a light scar, but you're tougher in the end. Also go back to chapter one to go over how to know if you're ready to date again.

Here are a few more tips in getting over your break up:

- Let out all those emotions. Cry away. Many people pretend to be "totally fine" with it all. "I'm okay. We just weren't meant to be." That is true, but we are human beings with emotions! This is not a sign of weakness. Cry all you need! This goes for men and women. Women are more okay about crying with others and men prefer in private, but it's so important to release these feelings in the form of tears.

- You may feel misunderstood and you may want to talk more and maybe get back together. Rarely does getting back together stick. This prolongs the hurt. Try to not beat yourself up as to why it didn't work out. More than likely, you were just not going to be a good forever fit (and more than likely you do know the issues that broke you up). Learn and find ways to move forward.

- If you dated a long time and were the most invested, don't suggest to just be real friends and hang out with all your friends. This gives the least invested one hope. I'm not saying that one day you can't be true friends but you just can't successfully do that while you're trying to heal from the break up.

- Don't fall into unhealthy routines to numb the pain. You'll probably feel numb without this (alcohol, drugs, over eating, sleeping with an old ex). Just feel numb and know this is part of the process of getting over someone. Hey, and no drunk texts, okay? "It couldn't hurt to send just one text... right?" Wrong! If he ignores you, it'll sting. If he does reply, you probably won't like the answer. You have to start the no communication timeline over again. Resist the temptation! Email it to yourself or your best friend instead.

- Confide in a good friend, therapist or family member to process how you feel.
- Listening to music has therapeutic effects. Whether you cry to that music (sappy love songs or break up songs) or sing at the top of your lungs, you'll feel better afterwards.
- Throw or pack away reminders of this person. Pictures, trinkets, special jewelry, love notes or anything else that reminds you of this past love.
- Journal your feelings. Write a letter (but, don't send it) to your ex to get out those feelings. It'll help you process how you feel.
- Be wary of a rebound relationship. Probably good idea to take a break if you just came out of a long-term relationship.
- Learn from the experience. Every relationship is full of lessons that can only be learned after going through it and reflecting afterwards.

- Once the intense pain is over, you can have the attitude that you're out of relationship with the person who is not right for you and you're now open and available for the one that is.
- "Pain is inevitable, but suffering is optional." This anonymous saying sums up another great way of thinking about your break up. Our mind controls our thoughts and decisions.
- Read the book *It's Called a Break Up, Because It's Broken.* A lot of great break up advice in this book!

Reflection Questions:

We've all experienced a break up before. What's the hardest part for you in getting over someone? After reading this, what will you do the next time to truly get over someone (maybe faster or more effectively?)

The hardest part of breaking up to me is missing the companionship & intimacy. No contact for a month or so I think will help in the future.

Chapter 12

How to Start a Single's Group

I'm the organizer/founder of the largest single's group in Louisville, Kentucky, called Singles Meet Singles, LLC (or SMS). As of this publication, the group has over 2,200 singles (age range of 40-65+). We are mostly filled with second- (or third- or more) time divorcees, some widow/ers and some never married. Forming SMS was a total accident because I was going to only have one party. I had met a large number of great men online that just weren't great for me and had a large number of great girlfriends and one day said, "You know what? I'm going to organize a party and invite all my new and past single friends and introduce everyone to everyone." So, because I was a teacher, I set the first one to be in June, once school was out.

All I did was make an event on Facebook (a great feature) and called it Singles Meet Singles. I made it a public event and gave the details in the event and asked all my single friends to, in turn, invite their single friends.

The first party was a great success, with 40 singles attending. Everyone said, "This is awesome. You *have* to do this again!" I hadn't planned on that but, since I was a teacher, it was easy for me to organize another event because I was off work all summer. For the second party, a friend had a deal at one of the bars downtown, so we hosted another—60 singles showed. There was a lot of dancing and mingling. At the third party, 90 people showed and by the fourth party, 110 people showed. (These were all at local bars where we could use their space, alcohol and music/dancing if available). After that fourth party I thought, "Wow! This is a NEED in the community! Everyone is dating off and online and is mostly 'one and done.'" So I made a closed/secret group on Facebook and let it ride. What a great way to connect other singles in the same age group and in the same age range.

I kept throwing/organizing parties/dances (all with good attendance telling me it must still be meeting needs). The goal of SMS is to connect to others traveling the same path, support where each is and find ways to serve in our community. When people serve others, deeper bonds are made. With each new party, people were seeing old, familiar faces as well as meeting a crop of new ones. Some dated in (or out of) the group. Most didn't. It was more about friendship and activity, especially for those newly divorced people who lost their married friends and needed something to do on the weekends when they didn't have their kids.

About a year later, my attorney friends said, "You should make this an LLC because your liability is growing" (we had alcohol at 85% of my events). I filled out the paper work and because I now had to pay taxes and expenses, I started charging five dollars for the parties I organized. This made some people mad (because before they were free), but I wasn't going to take all the expenses out of my school teacher/single mom pocket (no matter how passionate I was about connecting singles). I'd recommend this is you think you're going to have a lot of parties. If you don't become an LLC, you can give the money to charity. If/when you do become an LLC (if it grows along with your liability), people will already be used to paying a small fee.

SMS grew. People were driving up to two and three hours to attend these parties. I started a group in Lexington and Cincinnati over the next few years, throwing parties/connecting singles there. This helped them not drive as far to connect to singles and gave them a small group in their own city. But in December 2015, I closed Lexington and Cincinnati and just kept Louisville (it got to be too much because I was a mom, working, dating and after retiring from teaching in 2014, I had a few new life adventures on which I wanted to focus).

The main rule of the SMS wall is events only. (You can make your own rules). In between my big events (which are now only three times a year), anyone can make an event for others to connect. For example: NCAA game watching parties (as well as local college rivals and Super Bowl), day at the races, dancing, comedy club, bowling, movies, etc. I used to allow prayer concerns, motivational posters, cool articles, singles' discussions and hundreds of pictures, but the problem with that was all the events got lost down the wall. So I made it an events-only wall. Again, if you start a group, you can make your own rules. A few other things I've learned:

- I made a few policies and procedures and "rules" for the group so new people can see how we operate.
  - If I find out a person is dangerous (i.e. they went to jail for beating their wife, putting roofies in drinks, etc.), I take them out. No warning. Just out.
  - You'll find that singles don't like to commit until the last minute. (You know, in case they get a "better offer.") This makes it hard to let the bar/venue know how many are coming. I like to give a somewhat accurate number so they can have enough bartenders, etc. So just ask that they update their RSVP on the event a few days before the party.
  - You do have to continually monitor the wall for inappropriate comments or non-event postings. (EX: "Hi ladies... I'm new to the group—looking for a good time. Hit me up.") If you have Facebook on your phone, that's not a problem. It might also be good to have more than one administrator to help monitor this.

- I do provide nametags at my parties. This helps introduce people (especially if there are over 300 people there). I'm awful with names.
- When possible, I have door prizes donated to give out.
- I now have all my parties at a bar with a big dance floor and hire a DJ. I find that if you do fewer parties a year, more people come. If you do a party once a month, people just think, "Oh I'll go next month" (and probably won't). But, if you only have two to four a year, they're not as commonplace and I find attendance is better. The advantage of more people is simply it's a greater number of singles one can meet in one night.
- I give partial proceeds to charity. That can be your decision to do that or not. If you're not an LLC, you can have parties for free (or charge and give to charity only). But you do need to cover your costs of the venue, DJ, nametags, pens, etc. I only charge five dollars so it's a small cover for a four-hour party of 200-300+ singles and dancing.
- As the group gets really big, you'll find some people will find their smaller group, leave and do things on their own. Don't look at this as a bad thing. It's actually a good thing! They have found a group of people that meets their social needs and prefer a smaller group with whom to socialize. There are plenty of

new singles taking their place that are looking to connect to others.

- Is there drama? With any large group, you'll have drama. One might say, "There is too much drama in this group." The good thing is many times that person or those people leave the group (and suddenly the drama is gone). That is probably another advantage of having only a few parties a year.

- If you stay together over time, you'll have a few meet, get engaged and get married. That, for me, is the most satisfying part (aside from all the awesome new friendships). For people to actually have met because of the formation of the group and have a love connection; that is the goal of most singles, anyway... to find love again!

- Any leader of a large group will have some enemies. Not everyone will like you and the decisions you make. You need to have thick skin and know that the decisions you're making feel right to you. You will never make everyone in a large group happy.

- My Louisville group is a wonderful group of loving, giving people who like to give back. Over the years, we have helped serve the homeless (assisting an already established church group), helped tornado victims, given to needy mommas at Christmas time, etc. This brings people together in other ways than just having a party.

- One year I hosted a Single's Symposium. This is like a conference with a lot of offerings for singles to attend (finances, parenting and dating, internet dating, love languages, self-defense, etc.).

If you decide you'd like to start a single's group, I'd be happy to help you. Find me on my website www.loveand-laughterlifecoaching.com and I'll be happy to answer any questions over the phone. This has been a fun experience for us in Louisville and overall I'm glad it accidentally happened.

Reflection Questions:

Is starting a single's group something you think you could do? Who would you need to help you? If this is not your thing, can you think of someone who might do this for your community? Maybe you can be the behind the scene supporter?

Chapter 13

OTHER DATING TIPS AND TIDBITS

THIS CHAPTER WILL HAVE MANY different topics. Not enough for a whole chapter but, a lot of different topics and questions that come up in the dating world.

<u>Widows/Widowers</u>

As a widow, I can tell you, our path is a bit different than those that are divorced. We don't have the "ex" stories and usually no bad relationship stories. In fact, we seem to only remember the good times (knowing full well we all had normal ups and downs of a marriage). But we did not choose to be single, and now we are. Here are some common questions I have gotten:

1. How soon should I get back out there?

That depends on many factors. Do you have young kids that need day to day care? If so, there is so much to take care of that you won't have time (or probably won't want) to date. And you may have some guilt dating soon after. If your kids are older, then it becomes a little easier, but the people you meet just need to understand you're a full time mom/dad and don't get that every other weekend with no kids.

If you're an empty nester, you may be ready after your first year of "firsts" without him/her. If your spouse was ill for many years, you probably better mentally prepared for life after death. Some are never ready and don't wish to have another relationship. I think a lot of this depends on your age and where you are in life. But, don't listen to the judgments and opinions of others. You will know when it feels right to date. You can review the list of How Do I Know I'm Ready in Chapter 1.

2. *When do you take off your wedding band?*

Again, this depends on age and how s/he died as well as where you are in life. For me, I was 40 and quite young to be a widow. I waited three years to date and before I dated, I wore my ring on my right hand (to signify being a widow) about a year after he died. Once I started dating, I did take it off (or kept it on my right finger). And now, ten years later, I still wear it on my right finger for occasions such as his birthday, his death date, some events for our children (graduations, recognitions, etc.). For me, it was/is just a symbol that Wes is still with us. My kids also see that and remember he's there with us in spirit. After I remarry, I'm not sure how I'll proceed. Probably what feels right at the time.

3. What was the hardest thing for you with "getting back out there"?

Again, I'm sure this will be different for everyone, but for me, it was learning how to feel pretty/sexy again. I was used to my comfortable mom jeans and my ratty nighty, I needed to update my wardrobe. Also, because the dating world is so different, there is a lot of learn about how dating works the second (or third or fourth) time around. Hence, I wrote this book to hopefully help others. But, you definitely need to get a few dating outfits (widow/er or not).

For an older male friend of mine, he felt "judged" that he was dating too soon after his wife's death. (More about judgment in the next section). Only you know when you feel ready and remember: just because you go on a date doesn't mean you're going to get married. You're getting your feet wet and meeting new friends, trying to re-engage with a new social life. State your purpose for dating and that'll help. We all need to help educate those around us about how to look at singles who date.

4. What's the hardest thing about dating a widow/er?

One question many men have asked me is, "Are you looking for another Wes?" or in your case, "Are you looking for another like your deceased husband/ wife?" Most of us realize there will never be another like our deceased spouse, but we usually are looking for similar qualities/character in the one we date. That's what attracted us to them in the first place. The other tough part (and my father warned me about this when I started dating) widow/ers are the hardest to date. Many times the one we're dating thinks we're comparing him/her to our lost spouse. So it takes an extra amount of confidence to date us knowing we are just looking to find love again (just like a divorced person).

5. Do widow/ers have "rebound" relationships like some divorced people?

Actually, many do. A "rebound" is usually that first person you fall in love with after your divorce/ death of your spouse. But, this is all part of the learning. Just give your first relationship after time to grow. Don't forward think; just enjoy dating again.

6. Do you have any other advice for widow/ers?

I mentioned in "My Story" that I didn't know I needed therapy after Wes died, but I found I did. It probably wouldn't hurt to seek therapy after the death of your loved one to help you process a few things. It's a life changing, tragic event (especially if it was a sudden death). I personally think everyone needs a therapist and a life coach, so it certainly can't hurt you.

Don't compare to other widow/ers and their time frame. We all grieve differently and are in different places. I know several widows in their late 60s and 70s that don't ever want to remarry. That's okay, too. You must do what feels right for you. If it helps, process your feelings with a friend or a wise mentor.

Taking pictures down around your house depends on where you are with grieving, your age, and your kids' ages. For me, I kept pictures of Wes and me up for my children's sake. We have other traditions (hanging his Christmas stocking next to ours) and we'll quit doing those traditions when it feels right to stop. Many times you do just what feels right (for you and your situation).

Judgment in the Dating World

Oh my. This is a big beef with me. Probably because my dating life has been judged by a few and it didn't feel good. As singles, we are the worst with this. (Seems like the marrieds would be but, no. It's actually our single friends who are the worst!) Look—dating is about learning. Remember that 99% of the ones you meet will not be the one. Only ONE makes it in the end. That pretty much means that almost every meet will not be the one. Is it okay if you date someone for a month or two to get to know him/her to see if you're a match? Of course! How else will you know? Now, if you're with a different woman/man the following week or month, quit saying things like:

"Looks like she's his next flavor of the week!"

"Wasn't she just with someone different last week?"

"Man, he's a player because he has someone new with him every time I see him."

"He's been dating online for like seven years. Man, what's wrong with him?"

"She's a serial dater."

I could go on and on with the comments I've heard over the years. They're meant to be hurtful and make one look bad and not feel good. It's no wonder singles struggle with self-esteem and not feeling "good enough." So when I hear these comments I say things like:

"Hey, he's looking for love like the rest of us."

"He's dating online which means he may meet a lot of people but, I bet he will stop when he finds one he wants to date."

"She's a high-quality woman. She's just trying to find a high-quality man. There are not as many of them out there. Don't judge her for being on a date and discovering."

"Well it's not like she's sleeping with them all. She just meets a lot of new friends until she finds one she wants to date."

"Dating is 90% timing, and 99% of those dates don't work out, so it becomes a numbers game. At least she's remaining open and available. Good for her for putting herself out there."

Eph 4:29 (Read Florence, Littauers Boxa)

The point is to build each other up and not tear each other down. Don't always assume that a man or woman is sleeping with everyone because that's just not true. Some do and you'll find out who they are, but, still let him/her make his/her own mistakes. That's the best way to start rumors. Sometimes people just might be jealous that you have so many meets or dates and so to make themselves feel better, they're going to put you down to make you look bad. I've found most of the rumors in the single's world come from a place of insecurity or jealousy. In Corinthians 13:4, when it says, "Love is patient, love is kind. It does not envy, it does not boast, it is not proud." I'll remind you again what Andy Stanley says. "Envy means I don't feel very good about me so I'm going to make you not feel good about you." That is not love. So try to support more and judge less.

Brene Brown began her book, *Daring Greatly*, with Theodore Roosevelt's speech, "Citizenship in a Republic." The speech, sometimes referred to as "The Man in the Arena," was delivered in Paris, France on April 13, 1910. This is the passage that made the speech famous:

> It is not the critic who counts, not the man who points out how the strong man stumbles, or where the doer of deeds could have done them better. The credit belongs to the man who is actually in the arena,

whose face is marred by dust and sweat and blood; who strives valiantly; who errs, who comes short again and again, because there is no effort without error or shortcoming; but, who does actually strive to do the deed; who knows great enthusiasms, the great devotions; who spends himself in a worthy cause; who at the best knows in the end the triumph of high achievement, and who at the worst, if he fails, at least fails while daring greatly...

The reason I love this is it's not about the one sitting on the sidelines throwing judgmental swords at those singles who are in the arena. The opinions of those who are actually in the arena count. If you're in the arena of being single, you'll see that it's hard... hard to match each other's wants/needs and expectations. It's so much better supporting each other on his/her path and saying positive things and being there when a relationship fails (because most of them will fail). But in the end, there will be one that will emerge as a forever keeper and all the blood, sweat and tears will be worth it in the end!

Matthew 7:1 says, "Do not judge, or you too will be judged." For more on judgment, read my blog posted on May 16, 2015 called "Judge Less; Love and Embrace More," go to https://lewisloveandlaughter.wordpress.com.

Reflection Questions:

Have you ever felt judged before? By whom? What did you do? How can you better handle this in the future? If it was YOU who was doing the judging, how can you be more supportive in the future?

What's a Player?

Being called a player is an overused (and misused) word in the dating world. If you date online and meet a lot of people, are you a player? No. If you are casually dating a few people at a time, are you a player? No. If you jump from one relationship to another are you a player? No. Being a player means you have to be having sex with more than one person, but not telling the others you're doing so. *The Urban Dictionary's* definition is "a male who is skilled at manipulating ('playing') others, and especially at seducing women by pretending to care about them, when in reality they are only interested in sex. Possibly derived from the phrases 'play him for a fool,' or 'play him like a violin.'" Sex must be involved (with more than one) before one is truly a player.

A few ways to know if a man is a player is:

- Things turn sexual quickly.
- Poor track record for commitment.

- You more than likely won't be meeting his family or friends.
- He has a lot of female friends.
- He will call you hot and sexy.
- You'll only be introduced as his friend.
- He might disappear every now and then, but will surely be back if he's getting what he came for (sex with you).
- Focus on the surface—not many serious and meaningful conversations.

Can a player ever settle down? Surely. As soon as he finds one that will challenge him and is forced to chase you. But, until then, keep your eyes open so you won't get played. That's another reason to go slowly and observe his behavior over time. (Can a woman be a player? Yes. But most players are, by definition, men).

Baggage

Ah, how many times have you heard, "She has too much baggage," or "He has a truck load full of baggage," or "I can only handle enough baggage that'll fit in a carry-on bag"? Either way, everyone has some sort of baggage. Examples of baggage might be:

- Issues with an ex
- Mental issues like depression, moodiness or personality disorders

- Financial issues, debt, trouble paying child support or paying bills
- Troubles with children
- Troubles with career or maybe even unemployed.
- Childhood issues that are getting in the way of adult relationships (usually some form of abuse)
- Trust issues
- Lies
- Health issues
- Addiction issues (alcohol, drugs, porn)

The list could go on. Not all baggage is seen equally. What I mean is: to a single man with no kids, perhaps a woman with three kids implies baggage. Or to that single mom with three kids, she would not consider dating a man who has never been married with no kids. Here's the thing: You know how when you go to a yard sale and you find some treasure, the thing you've been looking for (the right size, the right color, shape, etc.)? Just like "one person's trash is another's treasure," the same goes for one's baggage in the dating world. The question is can you live with his/her baggage? We all have had issues in our past (especially the older we get). How was that baggage dealt with? Did s/he overcome? Is s/he still in the thick of it? How does s/he problem solve with these issues?

Just like dating is about learning, so is dealing with baggage. If we were to all throw our baggage into a circle, after looking at everyone else's baggage, we'd more than likely choose to keep our own. The baggage we carry around is our own. It's up to us to overcome and get to a better place so we can be better for someone else. Some can't do this on their own. Many need to seek therapy or hire a coach to move forward. So identify your baggage. See if there is a way to move beyond it and become stronger on the inside and then on the other side. If you can't, we just need to hope and pray that our baggage will be acceptable to our future partner and we can accept his/hers.

Gregg Michaelsen in his book, *To Date a Man, You Must Understand a Man: The Keys to Catch a Great Guy*, gives four ways to get his baggage exposed early. He said:

1. Meet his friends. If his friends respect him, they'll show this. If they are all players, he probably is too. Hit the road, Lucy. If he has lied to you, the truth may come out through his friends.

2. Meet his family. Observe how he treats his momma and siblings. Over time, they, too, may divulge valuable information.

3. Have your friends meet him. Many times they observe things we can't see. They can engage him in conversation and you can hear him verify stories—or not.

4. Get him drunk. "Alcohol is like a man's truth serum." A lot can be gained by listening to him when he's drunk.

Reflection Questions:
What would you identify as your baggage? Is this something over which you have control? It might just be that you need to change your attitude.

_____
_____
_____
_____

High-Quality Women

Have you ever met a high-quality woman? If you have, you know almost immediately after talking to her that she is a step above the rest. Here are a few traits you might find in a high-quality woman:

- She has confidence in who she is. She won't flip-flop with who she is with each man. She's the same woman with every person she meets.
- She doesn't have to have a man to be happy. She may enjoy dating you and you'd be proud to have her on your arm, but she is happy in or out of a relationship.
- She continues to work on herself to become a better person. In turn, she'll help you become a better person (and you'll be a better person just by knowing her). She'll be the biggest fan of your goals and pursuits (even if they are not her goals/pursuits).
- She has her own friends and interests and won't get jealous that you have yours. She's good with you each doing your own thing and is happy when you can spend time together.

- She likes to take care of herself spiritually, physically and emotionally. She'll be emotionally available in a relationship.
- She usually is grounded in her faith or higher power. This helps keep her humble, problem solve and helps her live in a state of gratitude.
- She's a good communicator and will treat you with respect (and will only be with you if you also respect her). She can be a good conversationalist with all she meets; either with idle chitchat or deep conversations about a variety of topics.
- She won't have sex with you right away. That is a treasure you'll have to earn over time.
- She's sincere and honest. You won't ever have to worry about her cheating on you.
- She'll make you feel comfortable when talking to her. She's down to earth, real and authentic.
- She can fit into any situation (i.e., not having a problem talking to strangers at your work party.) She can make good conversation and others will enjoy being around her.
- She will have nice manners and exude class.
- Her partying days are behind her.
- She has a mind and an opinion of her own. She won't always agree with everything you say, just so you'll like her.
- More than likely, her actions are filled with goodness and right intentions.
- She is filled with positivity.

This list might make her sound like a perfect woman. She may not have all the above traits, but definitely the majority of them will be present. She is perfectly imperfect, but she makes a point to work on those things in order to become a better version of herself. Obviously a high-quality man also looks for a high-quality woman. High-quality men and women are hard to find. But they are out there, so don't give up.

Reflection Questions:

For women: How many of these describe you? If the majority, you're a high-quality woman. Do you see yourself as a high-quality woman? Which areas could you improve to become more like a high-quality woman?

_____

_____

_____

_____

For men: Have you ever met a high-quality woman? How is she different from the other women you've met?

_____

_____

_____

_____

High-Quality Men

Now, onto high-quality men. You also will recognize a high-quality man after talking to him. He'll be "different" than most. You'll see there are similarities in the above list, but here is a list of traits a high-quality man may possess:

- Confidence is at the top of the list. He knows who he is and what he wants. He doesn't have to impress anyone because people will either like him or they won't.
- He is patient and knows it takes time to trust someone.
- He's always improving and he'll help you improve who you are.
- He's attentive to your needs. He'll compliment you and appreciate you.
- He's a good communicator. He'll text you after the date and tell you he can't wait to see you again.
- He won't participate in sexting. Because he respects women, he'll treat her with respect.
- He'll be respectful of you needing to wait before having sex (because, of course, he's dating a high-quality woman). He will honor your timeline.
- He is usually a family man. Not only with his own kids, but with extended family (and your family will adore him). If he doesn't have kids, he'll be good with your kids.
- He has good balance in his life: work, family, friends, home time, going out time and of course, time with you. He will make you a priority.
- He can have an emotional conversation with you as well as cut up and be light hearted.

- He also has a faith that helps keep him grounded.
- He has a life of his own and is enjoying it. Having you in it is a welcome addition.
- He cares about his appearance. He wants to look nice for all his interactions- you included.
- He's faithful and loyal. He wants to date only you. If it looks like you're not going to work out, he will have an honest conversation with you, trying to work things out and he won't veer.
- He's mature in his actions and thinking.
- He likes to remain positive and will only enjoy you if you're also positive (most of the time. We all have our low moments).
- He will make you feel special when you're with him.
- He will volunteer his time and help others.
- He lives within his means and will always take good care of you.
- He's honest and straightforward. He does what he says and will say "I'm sorry" if he's wrong.
- He's a humble man.

Again, you may be saying, "Where in the world is there a man like this?" They are out there. But again, they are hard to find, though they do exist. To women rearing boys, this is a great list to instill in your sons. Your future daughter-in-law will thank you.

Reflection Questions:

If you're a woman: Have you ever met a high-quality man? Would you like to attract a high-quality man? How can this man see you?

_____

_____

_____

_____

For men: How many of these traits describe you? If it's the majority of them, you're a high-quality man. Do you see yourself as a high-quality man? Are there areas you need to reflect/improve to be a more high-quality man? Are you looking for a high-quality woman?

_____

_____

_____

_____

The trick to attracting a high-quality man is to become a high-quality woman (and vice versa). Again, the Andy Stanley saying, "Are you who the one you're looking for is looking for?" We must be/become who we want to find us. Otherwise, they won't even see you!

The Push-Pull

The push-pull is a part of many early relationships and can sometimes go on for a year. For example, a man might feel a woman is getting too close too fast, and he will pull back (this might look like leaving more space between texts and seeing each other; becoming less emotional in his communication than he was before). This is a time he needs a little space and the best thing a woman can do is nothing. Don't say, "What's wrong?" and bug him for answers. He'll either be back or not.

If he comes back and gets too close to you, you may find yourself pushing him away. This goes back and forth until you come up with a pattern and understanding of each other. Sometimes the woman pushes back first (maybe she's uncomfortable with him being way too emotional in the beginning, or maybe she's feeling pressured to move more quickly physically than she'd like). Both women and men do the pushing and pulling. The thing I find helpful is to recognize and say out loud that this is a "thing" so when either person feels it happening, call it what it is, and you won't feel as abandoned and fearful.

If the push-pull happens often enough, you may reconsider the relationship. This can take you on an emotional rollercoaster. Maybe there are commitment issues on one side, or abandonment issues that need to be addressed (in therapy). A little push-pull is normal, but a lot of it is not good. Step back, pray, hope for the best thing to happen (and if things don't work out, learn from the experience).

Long Distance Relationships

What if the one you're dating lives miles away? Obviously, the closer to each other you are, the better (especially if it's within a two- to three-hour drive). Further than that, however, makes being together difficult. If you talk to anyone who has had a LDR, they'll tell you the most important factors in making it successful is trust and communication! No surprise, right? The same thing is needed if you live next door, but it's even more vital to have this with miles between you. Below are some great suggestions on making a LDR work:

- Having a fairly early conversation about if one would ever consider moving to you or you to them? (one day—not right away) If neither is willing to move (for whatever reason—job, kids, rules of divorce about taking kids out of state, etc.), then you'll have to decide if you have common purpose and desire to date this person. (For example: I dated a man that lived 2.5 hours away. He wanted to move back to Chicago and never drive a car again and I wanted to stay in Kentucky—in the suburbs—to be close to my children because I'm their only parent and my desire to be close to them was unwavering at the time). So, we parted ways as good friends because our future desires were so different. What became a 5.5-hour drive (for us after he moved to Chicago) was going to be too great to make it work if neither of us was going to be willing to move eventually.

- Another way to look at it is just date with the distance and see what happens. Focus on the relationship and not the distance. It's amazing what might happens if the two of you fall in love with each other. Maybe you can get creative with how to make it work or one might change his/her mind?

- Have conversations about each other's expectations. One partner might be good with seeing each other every weekend. The other might only want/need every other (especially if kids are involved with shared weekends).

- Agree to be 100% honest with each other. The goal is to make this work. There's no use lying to each other. The goal is to make the relationship last in the long run. Begin with the end in mind and start off on the right foot.

- Phone conversations—find a pattern of how much talking is good for you. Some may like every night, others every other or four nights a week? Make a date for it. Luckily, in the age of smart phones, this makes it easy to talk all times of the day, when driving and on the run. Also, FaceTime and Skype make it easy to see each other every day.

- You might have social media boundaries—liking, posting, etc. Everyone has different comfort levels with this. This might not be an early conversation, but definitely one that will come up later to discuss.

- Learn each other's schedule. You'll naturally do this over time. Saying good morning each morning and good night every night is the best way to start and end your day with each other.

- Watching TV or movies together over the phone is a new experience.

- Sharing pictures is also easy—taking selfies, Snapchat and Facebook all make this easy.

- I love words so I like this idea: share a journal. For a few weeks, you write in it—sharing feelings and dreams. Switch off the next time you see each other and let him write in it. What a great keepsake over the years when you're together in the end.

- This one is good if you both like to read—read a book together, especially if you both like the same type books. Read a chapter and discuss. Go at a pace good for you both. There are also great books like *100 Questions to Ask Before You Get Engaged* and others that serve as great conversation starters.

- Plan trips together. Do this not only to see each other, but to different locations so you can have a lot of time and experiences together to talk and discover.

- Send care packages!

- Send love notes over email. Or better yet, hand write one maybe once a month (i.e., the 14th of every month) and send them to each other. Keep them in a binder so you can reread them (for an added touch, spray your perfume or cologne on it so s/he can smell you too).
- Shop online together.
- For fun, when you're on the phone or Skype, write a song or a poem about each other together. It can be serious or silly.
- Watch the sunset or look at the moon at the same time, if you're in the same time zone.
- Find and take one of those online compatibility tests and share your results.
- Don't keep score with how many each texts or visits the other. One person might text more and one might travel more to the other. Again, you'll find your pattern over time.

Rejection

Ahhhhh... no one likes rejection, right? Not men nor women, but unfortunately, if you want to date, this will likely be something each of you will at some point encounter. Keep this in perspective. Here are some thoughts on the matter:

If a man asks a woman out and she says no. Well, she wasn't going out with him before he asked and she's not going out with him after he asked. So... nothing has changed (except for the saboteur in your head telling you what a dummy you are for asking). You have to keep asking! They won't all say no.

Think of dating like someone in sales. You might have to get 100 no's before you get a yes. You might think, "Really, ONE HUNDRED no's?" If you date for a while, it'll easily add up to this amount. BUT, when you get the yes, ahhhh, it feels so good. As time goes on, your approach will get better (just like in sales), you'll be a better reader of women and you'll get fewer no's and more yes's.

The rejection is not always about you. S/he may not be in the same place as you or has different preferences, so look at the rejection is a good thing. Now you're open and available for the person that *is* right for you. So the rejection many times is a blessing. (Although it doesn't feel like it at the moment you're getting the "No, not interested" or "I'm already dating someone," or "I don't think we're a match.")

You'll need to develop thick skin, especially if you're on-line dating. There are just so many choices and people with different preferences. They are not all going to like you and think you're a good match, just as they all won't be attractive to you and be a good match. It's a good thing God gave us the ability to discern.

Insecurities

No matter how confident you are, almost all of us have insecurities. We are too short, too tall, too fat, too thin, have a mole on our face, a birthmark on our chest, our hair is too straight or too curly, too bald; the list goes on! When I was in college, someone made a derogative statement about my thighs. Now, my thighs (in my opinion) have always been the worst part of my body so when someone made a comment about the cellulite on my thighs, it pretty much confirmed that my thighs are hideous. I carried that for many years and will still catch myself making negative comments about them, but the truth is no one really cares what my thighs look like. My *dazzling* personality, positive energy and character are way more important than a little cellulite on my thighs. A girlfriend of mine hates her upper arms. She won't buy or wear certain outfits because they show her arms.

I asked her, "Sally, do you care if I have cellulite on my thighs?"

She said, "What? No. I could care less."

I said, "Why?"

Sally said, "Because I love you and could care less what your legs look like."

I said, "That's exactly how I feel about your arms. YOU are the only one who cares. It won't affect how I or anyone else feels about you. Just like no one cares what my thighs look like, except me."

So, in the future, just be the best YOU that you can be and quit worrying about all the outward insecurities you have. (No one cares—except you).

Reflection Questions:

What is your biggest insecurity? Moving forward, how can you make this less of an issue?

Gratitude

You may have heard how important it is to live in a state of gratitude. I have heard this for years, and practiced this "when I remembered," but it wasn't until I watched The Secret and borrowed one of their ideas, that I actually started TRULY practicing gratitude every day! What do I do? I have a small rock/stone onto which I've typed/glued the word "gratitude." I put it in my pocket every morning naming something for which I'm grateful. Throughout the day as I touch it, I name another thing for which I'm grateful... at day's end, yet another. When I began, I just named things for which everyone says s/he is thankful (kids, family, friends, house, food, job, etc.). But after a while I started naming things I would not say in a prayer to thank God for (i.e. dry underwear, multiple pair of shoes, running water that can get hot or cold, clean pillow case, carpet under my feet). I always try to think of things I have not named before. This is how to truly live in daily gratitude. Then when things go wrong in life, I'm so used to being grateful that I see the blessings in the bad things that happen to me or my loved ones.

In August 2015, I got an eye cancer diagnosis (uveal melanoma that was treatable), but I was told I would lose some eyesight after the first year. Even for someone like me who lived in daily gratitude, you wouldn't believe how blue the sky was (the same sky I saw and was grateful for the day before). How luscious the trees and flowers looked. The air smelled fresh, clean and crisp (even with the humidity). I saw more people smiling when I smiled at them. My skin felt softer. I saw the good in everyone even though we all were not always good. You get the idea. Even though I was not going to become totally blind, how grateful I was for all my senses (especially my eyes to see). All of a sudden, all the petty things in the world fell away! Seriously, who cares if people make judgments, talk mean, if it rains when I want the sun to shine? Who cares if I'm cold with the AC set on frigid, if my muscles hurt from working out, if my jeans are a little snug or my wrinkles are increasing in number? I was/am so grateful for all of it.

All this happened because I got a cancer diagnosis (And I will survive. I am now cancer free). How many people do you know that have been diagnosed with cancer? (I feel sure almost all of us can name several persons right now). Or perhaps a different disease they have they didn't plan on having at an early age? I know there are so many with these diagnoses, partly because as I get older, my friends are also "aging" and new "diagnoses" are being discovered. But, oh, how lucky we are with advanced technology, great doctors and more advanced treatments. So when we look at our state of singleness, we will more easily embrace where we are in life if we truly live in a state of gratitude. Find a small rock/stone and start this habit. Share it with others.

"We cannot solve the world's problems at the same level at which they were created."
--Albert Einstein

For My Married Friends

If you're married, you may be reading this because you're my friend and are supporting the writing of my book or you're secretly thinking your marriage is on the rocks and you might want to sneak a peek at what the single life will be like if you divorce. Unless you're in an abusive relationship, I can't scream this loudly enough: "STAY MARRIED!" The grass is not greener on the single's side of town. I know it might appear to be fun and exciting, but the analogy I will use here is when your transmission goes out of your car: your car is shot; it won't run like it used to. You have to decide whether to get a new (used) car or pay a little extra money to get a new transmission. At least you know you've taken good care of the car you already have. You have gotten oil changes regularly.

It has been a good, reliable car for you. It's well made. If you get a used car, spending more than what a new transmission costs, how do you know how well it was made? How was it maintained? How do you know the transmission won't go out a month after buying that used car? So it's worth spending a little extra money on the relationship you have now (therapy, marriage enrichment, spiritual counselor, coach, pray, spicing things up) than it is to spend more and not know what you're going to get (divorce, someone else who may be broken or has had all sorts of problems, empty relationships, etc.).

<u>Saboteurs</u>

Let's talk a minute about saboteurs in relationships. This is one thing I work on with every client because we all have saboteurs. It's just a matter of how much power we give them. A saboteur is a noun that is fairly new to the English language; it was first used in the early 1900s, and it refers to a person who deliberately destroys or obstructs something. It comes from the French word, saboter, which truly means to kick something with an old fashion wooden shoe. The Merriam-Webster Dictionary defines saboteur as "a person who destroys or damages something deliberately."

Most saboteurs begin in childhood. Some emerge from past lovers. The negative messages we hear from our parents, relatives, teachers, past girl/boyfriends and friends stick with us into adulthood and we carry them into relationship. You may have learned that if you get too close, you lose yourself.

There might be abandonment issues or perhaps you were controlled by someone with whom you originally felt safe. You can see why our past experiences create fear in our future relationships. Sometimes we allow these saboteurs to get in the way. These behaviors become toxic and sometimes a relationship fails when it might otherwise succeed. Many of these behaviors are not intentional. We don't even know we are sabotaging relationships.

Periodically when we break up with someone, we give all the reasons why s/he was not good for us. But rarely do we examine and think it is we. It takes courage to look in the mirror and examine our part of failed relationships.

So how do we get past this? In Randi Gunther's book, Relationship Saboteurs, she gives seven steps to end your sabotaging behavior:

1. Be willing to look at your patterns without being self-critical. You most likely learned these patterns in childhood from people you trusted and have repeated them so often that they seem to be part of you. Look at yourself through the lens of a loving camera and just note what you see.

2. Look for where you learned those patterns and who the people were who taught them to you. Go as far back in your life as you can to find the external dialogues that you have now internalized.

3. Look for the trigger points in your present life that are likely to set off those unconscious behavior patterns that get you in trouble.

4. Pay attention to when those triggers are most likely to happen by being in close touch with your levels of vulnerability and resilience.

5. Look for people you respect and admire who behave differently in the same kinds of situations and note what they do differently. Then make a plan to try those behaviors instead of the ones you have practiced.

6. When you are trying to change, carefully select people who will support you in your attempts to find new ways to behave. Be careful of those who have an investment in your staying the same. They will knowingly or unknowingly counter-sabotage your efforts.

7. Create a plan to stay on track by caring more for yourself. Remember, every moment in your life your behavior will take you closer or farther from the person you are trying to become. Don't put yourself down when you slip. If you start living that new behavior again, you will eventually triumph over it and leave your sabotaging patterns behind.

Reflection Question:

If you had to name your saboteurs, what would they be? Give them a name. As soon as you recognize them, you can now give them less power.

The Missing Tile Syndrome

This is an excerpt from the book, *Happiness is a Serious Problem,* by Dennis Prager. This definitely relates to dating and it a good eye opener if you find yourself doing this, either now or in your past. I know I have done this in my past.

One of human nature's most effective ways of sabotaging happiness is to look at a beautiful scene and fixate on whatever is flawed or missing, no matter how small.

This tendency is easily demonstrated. Imagine looking up at a tiled ceiling from which one tile is missing—you will most likely concentrate on that missing tile. In fact, the more beautiful the ceiling, the more you are likely to concentrate on the missing tile and permit it to affect your enjoyment of the rest of the ceiling.

[...] I first learned about the Missing Tile syndrome from my friend Joseph. We were both single into our thirties, and we often talked about dating and women. The most recurring theme was our—especially my—search for the Most Important Trait in a Woman (MITIAW). I was obsessed with figuring out the MITIAW. Typically after a date I would call Joseph to announce what the MITIAW really was. After one date it would be personality, after another it was physical attractiveness, after another it was intelligence, and after yet another it was good values.

(I'm now paraphrasing) This went on for years until Joseph finally stopped him and made him realize that the MITIAW was the trait that was missing. He was embarrassed because he realized that Joseph was exactly right. There is no way every woman can have EVERY trait he wanted.

He said, "No wonder I wasn't finding a woman to marry. Since no human being can possess every good trait, every woman, by definition, was missing the MITIAW! If I truly wanted to find and value a woman, I was in a permanently self-destructive cycle."

This excerpt is a good reminder that we need to look at the whole person and accept the parts that are not perfect or *exactly* what we want. If you have a good 80% in common, I'm sure you can work around the other 20% and see if things can work out. If your meet is only 40-50% in your mind, then there might be more than just a few things that won't make him/her a good match. Remain open and quit focusing on the missing tile.

<u>Affirmations</u>

You may have heard about the power of positive thinking. I remember my father talking about this when I was growing up. Affirmations are similar to this, but more specifically, they are positive statements about yourself made in the present tense. The dictionary defines an affirmation as "the action or process of affirming something or being affirmed, also as emotional support or encouragement." This is an important aspect of the Law of Attraction. When reading this, you may think this is a silly practice. You may think this is only for women or for those with low self-esteem. While certainly helping low self-esteem folks, this is a good practice for us all: young and old, men and women. The purpose is to make you feel better, pour positive thoughts in your head, motivate and inspire you! They are always positive. You can repeat these affirmations whatever your circumstance. If you're sad, lonely, depressed, scared, fearful or stressed, you can tailor make the affirmations that will work for you.

If you don't repeat daily affirmations, why not start to-day? Write a few down. Say them in the present tense and say them until you believe them to be true! It's like studying for a test. You have to say the content over and over again in your head until you remember it. What can it hurt? No one else will know you're saying them. They will make you feel good after saying them because they are true statements about the real YOU!

Our mind (and the thoughts we put in it) is a powerful tool. If we fill our minds with more negative than positive, then that's what we'll draw to us. Here are some examples of affirmations:

- I am beautiful/handsome.
- I am a strong, confident person.
- I have a good body.
- I love my face.
- I am happy and full of joy.
- I am worthy and enough.
- God loves me and I love me.
- I'm successful and can handle conflict.

Let's relate this to dating. Before going on a date, it's great to say (out loud) all the things you know to be true about you. (The POSITIVE things about you). Here are some examples:

- I am full of love.
- I love me and everyone I meet.
- My relationships are long lasting and loving.
- My heart is open wide and I'm ready to love.
- Everywhere I go, I find love.
- Women/men are drawn to me.

So start today. Make a list of the top ten. Add to your list as needed. Start affirming the wonderful person you know that you are.

Reflection Question:

What are some specific affirmations you can start making today? Write them down here.

Dating Manual

This is an idea that may or may not resonate with you. Take it or leave it, but this is something I've found to be useful the few times I've used it. You know how when we have a baby and the parents wish each child came with an "owner's manual?" As new parents, we just are not totally sure how to parent our child. And when child number two comes along, that child is nowhere near like child number one and we have to parent them differently. Well, this is exactly the same way with dating. Each time I go out with a new man, he's totally different than the one I dated the last time or perhaps ever before. How I wish I had an "owner's manual" to know the best way to date him. How he wishes he could have an "owner's manual" of how to successfully date me. So, I wrote my own owner's manual of "How to Date Elizabeth Lewis." I can't say I've given it to every man I've dated, but only to a few who ask me if I'd like to be exclusive. (You definitely would not hand this out on a first meet! Yikes!)

Here are some ideas of what you might include in your owner's manual, if you so choose to write one:

1. How long you like to wait before having sex is a biggie. If that amount of time is too long for him to wait, he can choose fairly early on to move on. Or if he adores you enough, he now knows your standard and he'll have to wait for the "cookies." (Steve Harvey's verbiage).

2. How you prefer to communicate. Texts? Emails? Phone calls? And it won't hurt to ask him/her to not ever talk about anything serious over text. You can keep each other accountable with that.

3. Maybe something about your kids, like how long you wait to introduce. Or how you like to date with kids (your schedule could be explained if you're divorced and share children).

4. You might add a comment about church/faith and what it means to you.

5. Whatever you value, should be included. For example, for me I said, "I'll always be honest/transparent with you. I'll hope you'll do the same with me. If you lie to me, I'll probably break up with you. If I lie to you, you should break up with me. There's no room for deceit in a relationship." That makes it pretty clear about what will happen if we lie to each other and lets the man know it's a high value for me. (Feel free to copy it).

6. Any other boundaries or standards you may have (i.e. sleeping over, safety, drinking).

7. I also include this: if we're both dating online, we need to assume we're both dating/meeting others until we have the conversation that we're going to be exclusive and just focus on each other. Even if we both go off line (because I go off line a lot), that doesn't mean we have to go fast. I've learned that going slow is best. There are a lot of layers to peel away first to really get to know someone.

Again, it's best to keep this about a page long and share it only when it feels right (if you choose to do this at all). When a man asks to go exclusive, you want to make sure he can live with your standards, with how you like to date. (One of my clients wrote one just so she could be clear with what *her* standards were. She wasn't even sure when talking out loud about it). Each man I've given this to has liked it. Two men, in turn, wrote one for me to let me know what his standards were. I loved that too! There can definitely be great conversations around this. Since everyone wants to be successful with dating each other, why not give this a try?

Reflection Questions:

Can you think back to times you have identified The Missing Tile? Has it affected the way you think about the person you're meeting? If so, what can you do to stop this cycle?

_____
_____
_____
_____

What are some affirmations you can start saying today?

_____
_____
_____
_____

If you wrote a "How to Date You" manual, what would you be sure to include?

_____
_____
_____
_____

Chapter 14
DATING BOOK ADVICE WORTH SHARING

BECAUSE I WANT THIS BOOK to be *filled* with great and practical dating advice, I thought it would be a good idea to take ten dating books I have read over the last few years and share the highlights of them. If you find that one of the books is speaking to where you are right now with dating, buy it! I'll give the title and author and you can buy it/them on your favorite book-buying site. None of these ideas is my own (although I may have experienced or practiced many of these things). They all came from the respective authors. Giving a few highlights won't do any one book justice, but I found them worthy of sharing. You may ask, "Why put these authors' information in your book?" My answer is I want to help singles with many ways to look at dating and if great advice is already out there, I can help guide you to the source (just like I'd guide a client). So soak up all these great pieces of information (and again, please buy their books if you want to know more. I am only hitting the highlights of the parts I thought were most valuable).

Elizabeth B. Lewis

The 30 Day Love Detox by Wendy Walsh

To find out more about Wendy, go to Wendy@ DrWendyWalsh.com.

Dr. Wendy Walsh was kind enough to be on my radio show (Fall of 2015) so I read her book. She is a Doctor of Psychology and media commentator who is obsessed with the science of love. Her credentials and accomplishments are numerous (look at her website). I thought she had many good points in this book and I definitely wanted to share them with you here (I've already quoted a study that was in her book in Chapter 4).

Wendy talks about "The Backward Sexual Economy":

- About 50 years ago, men were married with a job and kids by age 27. Now, he may have moved back in with his momma and there is an abundance of women available to him. There are women his age dating, single moms and cougars—all vying for the same men. Your wild and crazy girlfriends are making it worse for you because they are enjoying their 'sexual freedom' with your future boyfriends.

- Wendy quoted, "A study of 117 countries shows that when men outnumber women, marriage rates go up. But when women are in oversupply, an oversupply of sex occurs and more children are born out of wedlock."

- Wendy breaks down love in four categories and explains each in her book: sexual attraction love, romantic love, intellectual decision love, and mature or companionship love.
- The not so good news about love is men can have sex with no emotional bond and women achieve that bond by having sex. She confirms (like so many other experts) that men and women fall in love differently. Men must have an emotional connection to fall. They also won't fall until they're ready. When he is ready, the one he is with at the time will be the lucky woman. Women have an increase of oxytocin when having sex and they fall in love more quickly than men. Do not assume that if you are ready, he is ready. If he says he is not ready, listen to him. You cannot talk him into this. He will be ready when he is ready.
- Wendy thinks casual dating is not useful. She teaches about attachment styles and insecurities. (There are tests you can take to see if one of these is you).
- The more short-term sexual relationships you have, the less you will be satisfied. We are impulsive with looking quickly through online dating profiles. This aids in shallow, short-term intimate relationships instead of taking our time to really get to know some-one.

- You need to have a relationship plan, just as you would have a financial plan or educational plan in school.
- She explains why living together prior to marriage increases the chances that you either won't get married or your marriage will end in divorce.
- She says there are Five Dominant Man Traits: (I am only going to list these. The book explains each in full).
  1. The Provider
  2. The Fixer
  3. The Thinker
  4. The Caregiver
  5. The Metrosexual
- The best part of the book is the "30 Day Love Detox," wherein she tells you exactly what to do. I'll only list her rules, but you'll definitely want to get the book to learn more about each of the items listed here.
- Purge all non-committed men.
- No sex!
- Remain calm and in control.
- Stop drinking if it reduces your resolve.
- Look for men who fit your relationship life plan.
- Buy her book to learn the following:
  1. The Advanced Detox
  2. The 10 Biggest Tech Mistakes Single Women Make

3. Your Attachment Style
4. Your Romantic Attachment Style
5. Sexual Relationship Style
6. How to Say No
7. When to Say Yes to Sex
8. How to Grow Trust
9. Training a Texter
10. Text and Attachment
11. The Porn Effect and Your Sexts

Boundaries in Dating by Dr. Henry Cloud and Dr. John Townsend

My weekly Life, Love and Dating group did this study in a ten-week series. You can buy the DVD and use the book to follow along with great lessons and examples. Dr. Henry Cloud is a clinical psychologist with a unique ability to connect with his audiences. Drawing upon his broad range of experiences in private practice, leadership consulting, and media, he simplifies life's issues and gives easy-to-understand, practical advice. John Townsend, PhD is an American Christian self-help author. Townsend co-authored 26 Christian self-help books during his career. I'm happy to share the high points with you. If this resonates with you, buy it.

- Boundaries define and protect us. They keep in the good and keep out the bad.

- The authors speak strongly about when there is deception of any kind, there is *no* relationship. In order to have a healthy relationship, there must be trust. They talk about the different types of lies. Absolutely do not tolerate any type of lying.

- If the person you're dating has trouble with conflict, "The Bible and all relationship research is very clear on this issue: people who can handle confrontation and feedback are the ones who can make relationships work."

- You should not figure out how to fit your spiritual life into your dating life; rather you should fit your dating life into your spiritual life. God can handle you asking questions, as well as asking for His guidance.

- In order to be happy with your dating life, it's important that you're first happy without being in relationship. You don't need to depend on another person for your happiness. You need to deal with your own insecurities, feeling lonely, fears, etc. before you can fully give to another human being.

- No matter how wonderful your upbringing was, or how smart and what an all-around good person you are, you still have to enter the dating arena and learn through trial and error—lots of lots of trial and error. Because we all sin, no one will be perfect and you will be let down.

- Basing every good relationship on friendship first is the way to go. Sex, attraction and romance are all great, but if there is not a solid friendship, then it's a rough foundation. Take your time. There is no reason to rush. Drs. Cloud and Townsend recommend dating a year (not including engagement) to be sure you have something more solid. They said two to three is okay, too.

- "We know that God has set up a time and a season for every activity under heaven (Ecclesiastes 3:1)." It's all about sharing a variety of experiences over time.

- I want to quote the authors here to be sure I don't get this wrong. "If you have hung around the church for very long, you have probably heard that God wants people to reserve sex for marriage. If you haven't and this is news to you, then I understand the shock you might be feeling. For many people, both inside and outside of the church, it does not make sense. If it feels so good, and is good for the relationship, and both people are consenting, then what is the problem? But what he begins with saying here is that sex is not a casual thing. It is holy, set apart for high purpose, and has *great value, dignity* and *esteem*. In fact, it is the highest form of expression that you can give another person of your romantic love for him. It is the highest value that your body possesses to give to someone you are in a romantic relationship with.

And, for that reason, like other things of high-value, to spend it casually or unwisely is foolish, and he will be cheated in the end."

Buy this book to learn more about boundaries on blaming and saying no to disrespect and *many* other lessons. This book is definitely worth a read.

Calling in "The One" Seven Weeks to Attract the Love of Your Life by Katherine Woodward Thomas

Katherine is an author and a licensed marriage and family therapist, and teacher to hundreds of thousands of people from all corners of the globe in her virtual learning communities. This book is *filled* with wonderful insight. It is recommended you go through this with a group. There are many great practice, exercises and study guides to assist you. Here, of course, are the parts that give you the best information. If this resonates with you, I'd highly recommend this book. To learn more about Katherine Woodward Thomas go to www.KatherineWoodwardThomas.com.

- In order to be ready to receive "The One" you need to resolve childhood issues. We all carry around wounds and until we address these, we won't grow stronger nor be ready.

- Katherine said, "Men and women, in general, have somewhat different needs. A woman needs to feel heard and tended to in a relationship. Ideally, she needs to be noticed, wanted, and adored. Men, on the other hand, need to feel needed. A man will thrive when he feels appreciated by his partner and when he is acknowledged for his accomplishments."
- The future love of your life more than likely will not look the way you think s/he will look. You have to look with your heart and not your hormones.
- Many say they want to move forward, but doing so causes fear and we'd rather suffer and move backwards then put ourselves out there.
- We need to learn how to experience loss and being disappointed. Experiencing loss is just a fact of life. It will happen to us all. So we need to know that nothing is actually wrong with us. We just need to experience this loss and move on.
- When we do decide to move forward and find ways to improve, we first might experience a loss. The loss of the old you. Things might get worse before they get better. Any time we choose to grow, we will lose a part of ourselves to make room for the new you to shine through.
- Our past may be filled with wounds. It's part of our story that is real and truly happened. But our "woundedness" does not have to be part of our future.

It does not have to define who we are now. We can learn from this woundedness and become stronger or remain a victim of our past.

- Katherine said, "Look at your life. What you have is a reflection of what you believe you can have, and relationships are a perfect mirror of your relationship to yourself. Love attracts love. We don't necessarily get what we want in life—we do, however, get what we give our attention to. We get what we believe we can and should have." Believing that love is possible for you will help with bringing love to you.

- I love this so much I want to directly quote her: "Practice unconditional acceptance of your life today just as it is, and make a conscious choice to be happy whenever possible. Every time you feel you're so frustrated, disappointed, and restless today, thank God for your life, exactly as it is and exactly as it is not. Affirm the goodness of your life whether or not you are getting what you want at any given moment."

- It's easy to not pay attention to all that goes on around us because of all the distractions; all that we're supposed to know and getting pulled in every direction. This makes us disengage from others.

- Love will be void from our lives if we don't allow love to generate within ourselves. If our Prince Charming doesn't show up, we get down and depressed. What we give will come back to us. We have to quit putting ourselves down (and others). Great people attract other great people. All the great ones are not taken. If you keep working on being the best *you* that you can be, you will not attract a negative, poor character or offensive person.

- We don't know when love will find us so it's important to remain open and curious. Think about having meaningful encounters with everyone you meet. Just know that it's getting closer.

- This is a great closing. Katherine said, "As the farmer who has planted his crops does not go out to his garden and tug on his plants in an effort to force them to grow, we wait. It is an active waiting, not a passive one, knowing that 99% of all creation takes place beneath the soil. We stand ready and alert. We till the ground. We know that the miracle is coming and we receive that miracle now. And together we say yes, yes, yes, and yes."

You Lost Me at Hello: From Dating to "I Do" by Jess McCann

This book was written by one of America's top dating coaches. Author and Dating Coach, Jess McCann has helped thousands of single men and women find love and relationship happiness. Through her proven coaching techniques and experience, Jess can help you quickly identify the answer to your question, "What am I doing wrong?" To learn more about Jess McCann and how to buy any of her books, go to www.jessmccann.com. Below are the parts I thought you would find most useful.

- Jess used to train sales people before becoming a dating coach. She cleverly related sales to the fundamentals of relationships.

- Like in sales, you're the most important "product" and it's important to start prospecting. This starts with hello. Be mindful with how you handle yourself with everyday circumstances.

- With early dating, you have to use your head as much as your heart. Don't let your emotions get in the way of making decisions. These decisions (like maybe just sending just one text or rearranging your life to see him) might turn him off even though it felt like the right thing for you to do at the time.

- If the results you're getting with every guy are the same, it's you, not he. You need to stick to (and be strict with) a dating strategy to get what you want—especially the more you're craving a relationship. This strategy would be like having a plan when looking for a new job. You're not just going to go with the flow and see what happens.

- Just as in sales, relationships take time; time to grow and get to know. And you can't sell a product that you don't like. So if you don't like yourself (you are the product), you won't get many sales. You need to love you first before anyone else.

- Do not follow the same routine. Change it up. Smile. Emit good energy. Try online dating.
- "If you stop prejudging, you will start dating."
- When you sell houses, you can't just sell one at a time. You always need to have a few going at a time because they don't all end with a sale. The same goes for dating. Don't shut everyone else out just because you found one that you like. You don't know if that one will work out in the end. There's nothing wrong with dating several at a time (until you become exclusive).
- This is SO important and I think this (and the next point) is one of the best parts of this book. We women have to look at a man's "buying signs." A man will have low interest, moderate interest or high interest. Women say it's confusing but it's not. If a man comes after you and then drops off communicating and asking you out, there is no confusion. He went from high interest to being moderately interested or to having low interest. If he stops chasing you, do not chase him back. If a man gets your number, but does not call, that is low interest. If he calls, texts, asks you out- that's high interest. We may not like the signs we're getting, but they are usually very clear by his

actions. That is why we should let a man pursue. We will be able to read his buying signs. And yes, his interest can change overnight (as can ours). If you are not getting high buying signs, move on.

• I think the next best take-away of this book is this: when we are on a date and things are going well, we should leave at the "Height of Impulse." Yes, even if sparks are flying around the room and you want to move the date to the next location, then *that* is when you should leave. Leave him/her wanting for more (a great way to increase your chances for a second date).

• Men will not respect women who have sex too soon. Why give the most important part of yourself to someone you don't really know? If he's only moderately interested, having sex won't make him highly interested. It's usually the other way around. Slow and steady will always win the race in dating.

Mars and Venus on a Date by John Gray, PhD

Like all the other books in this chapter, I am sharing some of the high points in which you may benefit. John Gray is the leading relationship expert in the world. His relationship and health books have sold over 50 million copies in 50 different languages in 150 different countries. His groundbreaking book, *Men Are from Mars, Women Are from Venus,* is the best-selling non-fiction book of all time. John helps men and women better understand and respect their differences in both personal and professional relationships. His approach combines specific communication techniques with healthy, nutritional choices that create the brain and body chemistry for lasting health, happiness and romance. His many books, videos, workshops and seminars provide practical insights to effectively manage stress and improve relationships at all stages of life and love. I will begin with John Gray's Five Stages of Dating. They are explained in depth in the book. If you are interested in this book go to www.Marsvenus.com

- He identifies "The Five Stages of Dating":
    1. Attraction
    2. Uncertainty
    3. Exclusivity
    4. Intimacy
    5. Engagement
- John explains, "There are basically four kinds of chemistry between dating partners: physical, emotional, mental, and spiritual. Physical chemistry generates desire. Emotional chemistry generates affection. Mental chemistry creates interest. Spiritual chemistry creates love."
- In the attraction phase, we need to get to know someone so we can give it a chance to grow, although it is okay to still meet others.

Elizabeth B. Lewis

- Once you really like someone and go exclusive, one of you might start having a few doubts. Many break up when this happens, but it's actually a natural phase to go through. Men tend to visualize the perfect mate and wonder if this one is she. This "perfect person" picture eventually disappears and the reality of this "real person" comes to light. This is the state where it's best to stay and see what can become of this relationship. This is where you will find the push-pull we have talked about earlier in the book.

- In the exclusive stage, the pursuit is not over. It has just begun. You need to focus on being the best partner to the other. If you become physical or emotional before you work on the mental or spiritual, the men usually pull away and the women become needy.

- I think this is one of the most important points in the book, so I'm going to quote John Gray. "Why is waiting (on sex) so important? Through fully experiencing stage three, men and women are able to move through all four doors to intimacy. When a man eventually tastes the fulfillment of experiencing complete physical intimacy with someone with whom he also shares emotional, mental, and spiritual intimacy, he cannot go back. Just to have sex when he could make love is like eating junk food when he could have a Thanksgiving feast. Why settle for less?

It may take more time and energy, but it is real and lasting. By taking the time to move through all the five stages, a man ensures that when he does give all of himself it will yield the greatest return."

- It's important to go through each stage in this process, respecting each stage. If one is more eager than the other, the process become restricted. There is much insight to be gleaned by going through every stage. If you find your relationship going too fast, it's best to move back a stage. This is hard to do. For example, married couples who separate are moving back to stage one or two. So try to go slow and hit every stage.

This book is filled with more great information/examples. It's definitely worth a read if it resonates with you.

*It's Just a F***ing Date* by Greg Behrendt and Amiira Routola

Greg Behrendt is an author and comedian. Amiira Routola is his wife and besides co-authoring with her husband, she writes a fashion blog called Outdress the Enemy. I can't say I like the title of this book because I don't like the "F" word, but it has some good dating advice I'd like to share with you. I reviewed this in my Life, Love and Dating class and we had some rich conversations. Buying this book will give you proper perspective and a lot of great, dating advice. Here are a few snippets of information you will learn by reading this book:

- The information in this book is very straightforward about the realities of dating. I've already quoted part of this book in my "Perspectives in Dating" chapter. It's just a f***ing date, not a commitment beyond that. So just go and enjoy.
- They say it's important to have a dating strategy and stick to it. No more "quasi dating, non-dating and hanging out." If you'll settle for a "hang out" then a "hang out" is what you'll get. Your time is valuable so wait for a real date.
- Men know they are supposed to ask women out. Yes, a woman *can* ask a man out, but men know they're supposed to step up and ask. So they suggest that the women flirt and let it be known you want to be asked out, and then let the men do the asking. If a man likes you, he *will* ask you out.
- They also believe you should not have sex right away. Or if you want to have casual sex, it's easy to find. You have to decide if you want to be "that girl." This is something that should be earned over time, if you want the relationship to move forward.
- If a date doesn't go well, it's not all your fault. You are only in charge of your half of the way the date went.

- When you have an active, busy life and are a "winner," others will be attracted. People also like movement. This is the way you move throughout your daily activities.
- They tell the difference between standards and deal breakers. "Standards are about how you live your life, where deal breakers are about how you view theirs." They give lots of examples so it's easier to understand.
- After a date, you might think you know how things went, but in reality you only know how YOU felt about the date. You don't know what the other person thought. This can be disheartening because maybe you thought it went great and how could he/she think it went differently? The best thing for you to do (ladies) is to just sit back and relax. Wait for him to reach out and ask you out again.
- If you do get the second date, you'll be more relaxed because you already know you like each other, but going back to his place for dinner and Netflix is not a good second date option!

Marry Him: The Case for Settling for Mr. Good Enough by Lori Gottlieb

Lori Gottlieb is the *New York Times* bestselling author with this title. The information learned here has a surprising look at modern love, marriage and what really matter for true romantic happiness. This book came along at exactly the right time for me for where I was with dating. Remember when I told you I went to therapy to get "unstuck" with the death of my husband issues? I read this book at the same time. It spoke to the many dating mistakes/mindsets I had while early dating. If you consider yourself "too picky" this might just be the book for you. I highly recommend this book. Here are the highlights that definitely helped me. I hope they help you, too.

- This book is about a gal who went to her dating coach (Evan) and was talking about her long list of what she wanted in a man. He helped her broaden her options of what she would except in a mate. As she was working with this coach and going on dates she was also talking to her girlfriends, who were also dating. These girlfriends seemed to be turning away all the 8s and 9s. Why? Because they were looking for the 10. What she realized, over time, is that the 10 really does not exist. The 10 is a manufactured person they have made up in their heads. (This was me in my early dating). Ten years later, she found her friends were still turning away the 8s and 9s (good enough who do exist) because they were still looking for the 10 (Prince Charming who does not exist)! Those same 8s and 9s were now happily married. My personal takeaway after reading this book is maybe we find and date an 8 or a 9 and over time you will morph that into a new 10. A real 10. One that is the right match for you on all levels.

- Many women end up single and miserable because they say they'd rather be alone than settle. Lori says don't start with your list because when you do that you find all the negatives in the person. Instead, go out with someone you enjoy and see where it goes. Throw away the idea you're going to get swept off your feet.

- Online dating gives us too many options. As soon as you email a person of interest, the site pops up pictures of others' profiles saying, "If you like that one, maybe you'll like this one?"

- Lori quotes from the book *The Paradox of Choice: Why More is Less*, by Barry Schwartz (which I have also read) and it explains the difference between maximizers and satisfiers like this (I will quote because Schwartz says it better than I): "Say you want to buy a new sweater. You decide that it needs to be well-fitting, stylish, not itchy, a pretty color, and in your price range. Say it even has to go with a specific outfit. Satisfiers walk into a store or two, find a sweater that meets all of these criteria, and buys it. She's done. A maximizer, on the other hand, walks into a store, picks a sweater that meets all of the criteria, and thinks, *this* sweater is nice, but maybe I should look at that cute store down the street. Maybe

I can find something I like better. Maybe I can find something on sale. So the maximizer hides the pretty sweater on the bottom of the pile (so that nobody else buys it) and goes to check out another store (or five). Now you might think that the maximizer will end up with a better sweater – after all, she's looked at more possibilities – but that's not necessarily the case. A satisfier isn't looking for the absolute best, but she does have high standards. The difference is she stops when she's found something that meets those high standards."

- Most women will say, "I'm not going to settle." They believe the longer they search, the better man (sweater) they will find. They think that finding a man that is only 80% of their "list" is settling. Over time, they realize it is better to choose the "good enough" guy round one.

- Obviously, a sweater isn't a relationship, but the principle is the same. Maximizers are going to keep looking for a better potential partner and choose no one, and satisfiers are okay when they find what they want. Lori says, "Satisfiers tend to be happier in life than maximizers. They're happy because they know that good enough *is* good enough. They realize that nothing is perfect in life – not jobs, not friends, not sweaters, and not spouses – so taking a good available option and appreciating it makes sense."

- Maximizers look back years later wishing they had what satisfiers have but it's too late. They could have had it, but they kept looking for that ten. "It's about finding someone who is *enough*, as opposed to someone who is *everything*."

- Lori believes women need to recognize that even one friend can't satisfy all our needs. That's why we have many friends. This is not to say we should have many partners, but it's too much pressure to think that one person can meet your every need.

- I'm quoting Lori again here because I think this point is KEY! "I'd read the same thing on the relationship expert Diane Sollee's smart marriages.com website: 'Research has shown that every happy, successful couple has approximately [ten] areas of 'incompatibility' or disagreement that they will never resolve. Instead the successful couples learn how to manage the disagreements and live life 'around' them – to love in spite of their areas of difference... If we switch partners, we'll just get [ten] new areas of disagreement."

Did you see yourself in any of these examples? I surely did. It really made me rethink the way I choose men. I know I have turned many good men away in my past because they were not everything on my "list." I was looking beyond my 8s and 9s looking for that 10... the 10 that didn't exist. I was basically looking for a handsome, clean-cut Jesus in my age range, in a starched button down and blue jeans; lesson learned. I highly recommend this book if you find yourself not giving nice men a try or think you're being too selective.

To find out more about Lori Gottleib, visit her website at www.lorigottlieb.com

Was it Something I Said? The Answers to All Your Dating Dilemmas by Jess McCann

This book is the second of Jess McCann's that I'm reviewing. I think it is filled with all sorts of questions that many ask about dating. I'm only touching the surface of all the great advice that is here. I think this is definitely worth a read. To find out more about Jess McCann go to www.jessmccann.com.

- Because we live in an instant gratification world and have our cell phone at our fingertips, we miss out on the ways dating used to be "pre-Internet." We were not as available. We had to wait for a man to call us on the phone to ask us on a date. But now we can communicate with someone half way around the world or quickly find out where someone is. Women think that if we don't answer a man right away, he might lose interest and move on. When in reality, it makes him want you more. Jess said, "That which makes you more available will also make you less desirable."

- Jess also believes that the man should make the first contact. This is how you will know his interest in you. She said you should be unpredictable with your responses. Maybe 30 minutes. Then an hour or even a whole day. She says this keeps a man on his toes.

- If you've been out with a man a few times, and then he quits calling, she said do not reach out with the "I'm just checking in. How are you?" text. This means, "I haven't heard from you. Where have you been?" The more he tries to see you, the more he likes you. If this stops, he's changed his mind. She said to lower your "textpectations." If you text him too often, he will become even less interested.

- When a man drops off communication, there almost always is another woman involved. If he has moved on, you should too.

- She says on a first date, the man should pay (for gay men, the one who does the asking should pay). It's okay for a woman to grab for her wallet, but if he lets you pay, you can let him go. Gentlemen should pay on the first date. After a few dates you can offer to maybe leave a tip, buy ice cream later or a drink before.

- If a man calls at the last minute, he is not interested in dating you. He is the non-committal type. A man

Elizabeth B. Lewis

that is looking for a long lasting relationship will plan
ahead and ask you out in advance.

- She also believes in waiting for sex. To know how
a man really feels about you, he has to really know
you. If you kiss a man before going on an actual date,
you're telling him he doesn't really have to "date you"
to "hook up" with you. She said, "If you don't feel
your hearts and minds are connecting, your bodies
shouldn't be either."

- In her book she will teach you the best way to handle
conflict when a man is angry with you.

The Sacred Search by Gary Thomas

Gary Thomas is a bestselling author (of numerous books)
and an international speaker whose ministry brings people
closer to Christ and closer to others. I thought this was good
advice for Christians dating. Quoting/summarizing snippets
of this book will barely touch on the many lessons packed in
these pages. To find out more about Gary and his other books,
go to http://www.garythomas.com.

- The goal of Gary writing this book is to make sure
you're crying tears of joy after ten years of marriage
and not painful tears.

- He says don't ask "who" will I marry; ask "why." You need to know why you want to get married before you decide who to marry.
- Don't get caught up in romantic foolishness. Stay grounded in Christ and use your church, family and smart friends when making decisions about love.
- Gary points out, "The Bible does not say follow your emotions, insist on thrilling romantic attraction that makes the relationship fun, and then all things will be added unto you." Rather, Matthew 6:33 says, "Seek first the kingdom of God and his righteousness, and all things shall be added to you." Gary says if you let God guide your path and don't compromise, then you'll end up in a more satisfying marriage. Don't follow cultural norms of romantic attraction and sexual chemistry. Romantic attraction is stronger than one's sex drive. Recognize that this is going on. Making a marital decision based on these is foolish.
- The infatuation goes away in about two years, maybe a little less or more but that's about how long our brains can stay smitten. The Bible says in James 3:2, "We all stumble in many ways." Gary says don't marry him until you see how he stumbles.
- Whether you're younger or older and remarrying, don't take shortcuts with getting to know each other. Your brain does not work properly when you're "in love." Listen to your family, friends and pastor. Even

a 55-year-old woman is like a 16-year-old girl when she's in love. If you decide to marry in less than a year, at least have the blessing of older, wiser friends.

- Care about your partner's godliness. Rarely do couples with marriage problems complain about his/her looks. It's usually character issues. So work now on becoming the right person and marry someone with a solid core.

- Your marital choice is important, but it won't define you. God defines your life, not your spouse. You do need to know the true character of the one you're marrying, even though who you pick won't define you.

- A good relationship is something you make. You don't just find it. You find a cell phone or you find infatuation. A sense of oneness with each other and God is something you make and it takes time. Three-way communication with God in the center is the way to go.

- Gary also says wait until marriage until you have sex. If you don't, it will make a break up hurt more and will dull your sexual connection with the one you do marry. He said, "God *designed* sex to be pleasurable and satisfying. He knew what he was doing, and no surprise, he succeeded. Sex can indeed be amazing. It's also a skill that can be learned, and that's what marriage allows, so if the two of you aren't 'compatible' on your wedding night, you have a lifetime to get there."

• Some believers want to wait for a "sign" from God to determine whom to marry. God will not pick your future partner. You get to pick.

• Glorifying God is the primary goal of life, not being in a happy marriage.

• He ends with this, "Are you dating with integrity? In your pursuit of a good marital match, are you acting with grace and kindness? Is the *process* of your search honoring God? While Jesus never dated, he did have friends, and his friendships reveal the nature of his relationships in such a way that we can imagine how he would date."

It's Called a Break Up Because It's Broken: The Smart Girl's Breakup Buddy by Greg Behrendt and Amiira Routola-Behrendt

"When one door of happiness closes, another opens; but often we look so long at the closed door that we do not see the one which has opened for us."
– Helen Keller

This is the second book I've reviewed by Greg and Amiira. This is a great book to guide you through a break up. I do think there are so many great points in this book and if you're struggling with a break up, it would be a good one to buy. Here are the key points I found helpful while helping others navigate a break up.

- You *will* survive this break up and more than likely you know why the break up happened (well, because there was something in the relationship that was broken). You can make the agony of this break up go on and on forever, or you can follow their advice and get over it quickly. Boy/girlfriends come and go. That's a fact of life. Just like some friendships come and go. That may not help the pain right now, but everyone at some point endures this. This pain won't last forever. You're still a great person and you *will* love again.

- The person who broke up with you decided that you're just not "The One." The one who did the breaking up is going to move on. You should, too. So no drunken texts, stalking his/her normal routine (you know so you can "accidentally" run into him/her). No stalking on social media. You have to go cold turkey. Get rid of his/her stuff if any is lying around the house. They say give yourself eight weeks to get over this person. If you still need to talk about it every day after that, then seek counseling and give your friends a break (they'll only tolerate so much listening to your broken heart).

- When the breaker-upper says, "I hope we can be friends. Or let's stay in touch," s/he doesn't necessarily mean that. It may be just a nice thing to say so s/he can quickly get out of break up conversation.
- If you find yourself being a hermit crab and staying home and hiding, wallowing in self-pity, call your friends and force yourself to go out. Remember you're a catch (that just needs to be caught by the right person). Always look good when you leave the house just in case you run into your ex. You don't want to be caught with no makeup and sweats should you see him.

If you like the points here, there are many more in the book. You can buy this book at your favorite online book ordering website.

Reflection Questions:
Which dating advice (in Chapter 14) helped you the most?

_____
_____
_____
_____

Which book(s) would you benefit from reading and learning more?

_____

_____

_____

_____

What is another great dating book you've read and want to share with others? (I'd also love for you to share you book reviews with me of other good dating books).

_____

_____

_____

_____

Chapter 15
PULLING IT ALL TOGETHER

THERE YOU HAVE IT. YOU'VE read everything I've learned, you've reflected on your own dating life, and read the highlights from ten dating books. There are hundreds of great books out there on relationships. Keep reading and sharing with others what you've learned. If you think about it, here are the common themes and key learnings:

1. WAIT as long as you can for sex. If this was not glaringly evident, I believe this message was in every book I've read (both here and the majority of the other books I've read). Why is this the #1 mistake in the dating world? It is only through trial and error, prayer, reflection, reading/learning, etc. that makes one rethink the whole right decision to make.

2. Men are hunters and women are gatherers. This is not just an old-fashioned philosophy. This is still a real deal.

3. Do not pressure a man. Let him move at his own rate. He will only be ready to settle down when he settles down. Hopefully that'll be when he's dating YOU!

4. Men and women don't communicate the same way, move at the same pace or operate the same way. It is a dance that requires both of you working together so you come out strong as a couple.

5. Dating is like being in sales. You have to love your product (you); know what you want; have confidence about it; properly talk about it and a quality product will sell itself.

6. Dating is about learning. The more you date, the more you learn. It is important to reflect on the things you have learned and it is best done with a support group and/or a coach.

7. There are many ways to meet the opposite sex. Date online and/or offline, you have to remain open and available to be found. Use all the resources available to you. It usually doesn't happen overnight. It takes effort.

8. Being confident and positive are the best ways to present yourself in daily living. Find ways to stay positive and not drown in the pool of negativity.

9. Do not rush the stages of dating. Discover your date and don't decide so quickly.

10. Be honest and loyal once in relationship. Lies will follow you and will always demote you.

11. Stay positive. Live a full life. Learn to love the "you" that you are (imperfections and all).

12. There is no ten or perfect person. We manufacture a future mate in our heads that is not real. Look for a good enough type of match and in the end you will be satisfied and then turn it into something terrific.

13. Porn and "Friends with Benefits" are never good behaviors if you want future success with finding "The One."

14. Reflection is key! Take ownership with your part of the unsuccessful relationship. Time between relationships is just as valuable as when in relationship. Learn from your past mistakes and throw those learnings into your next relationship.

15. Most meets/dates will *not* be "The One" so keep going out. Remain open and available. Learn. Have fun. Figure out what you like and don't like.

16. Do not judge other singles as they figure out the best path for themselves. All singles are in different places with dating and there is so much self-discovery that has to happen. Build up each other instead of gossiping and tearing down each other.

17. Slow and steady wins the race. Time will expose you or promote you. Every. Single. Time.

18. Do not give the silent no. Being kind and honest is something everyone can do and will make the journey a lot more fun and bearable.

19. Know your worth and trust your gut.

20. Do not take online dating personally and remember it's not the online site's fault if you have a bad experience. The site just helps you get meets/dates. It is up to you to screen and make better decisions about who you meet.

21. This next statement is true in life as well as dating (my brother taught me this): People ONLY spend time with people they want to be with. If a man wants to spend time with you, and you want to see him, you will both make it happen. If a friend or family member really wants to see you, they/you will make sure that happens. If they don't, it will not happen (except out of obligation or guilt). So observe who you actually spend time with and who tries to spend time with you. Those are the people that want to be with you.

22. Dating should be fun. If it is not fun, it is time to take a break.

23. Being needy is the most unattractive trait in a man or a woman. Confidence is the most attractive quality.

24. Making boundaries is always a good practice. Figure out yours and live by them. Don't compromise.

25. A lot of choices make it hard to choose. Only juggle a few at a time and stay available until someone pulls you in and asks you to be exclusive.

26. Falling in love requires being vulnerable.

27. When someone shows you who s/he is, believe him/her. Don't justify.

28. Finally, do not give up. Everyone won't find "The One" overnight or in a certain amount of time ("your" timeline). When you get discouraged or have a bad experience, surround yourself with positive people and those who are engaging life. Keep your head above water and don't drown in self-pity and kick yourself until your self-esteem is in the sewer. Find ways to get happy with yourself and your life, and the ones that do not last won't affect you as negatively.

So, why is dating the next time around so different/difficult? I believe it's a variety of reasons.

1. We now have past life experiences that have changed our mindset. It's not a priority like it was when we were thinking about having babies and making a family.

2. Some have fear of loving again. If you were cheated on (trust issues), struggle with rejection, lost a spouse and think your next mate may leave you (abandonment) or any negative relationship issue in the past, it's hard to move forward. Seeking professional help with this is not a sign of weakness. It's a sign of strength, and almost always you'll come out stronger for having gone.

3. Many of us have had children and we now have different priorities.

4. Some of us have not healed from past relationships and until we work on ourselves and become more whole, we can't be whole for someone else.

5. Some of the baggage singles carry around is heavy and only therapy can lighten that load.

6. If we have different future desires, it's hard to move forward with someone who may not want to go where you want to go (or support where you want to go).

7. There are too many choices. If there is one thing you don't like about someone, no worries. There are thousands more you can find either online or around the corner. This makes it harder to stick with one to see what they're all about.

8. Some live with a scarcity mindset. They worry about what they don't have and doubt that there is going to be anyone who can love them.

9. We are too quick to decide. We feel like our life is going fast, we are older and we want it all to happen now. Instead, we need to learn to discover and just enjoy the ride.

This last bit came from the book, *The 12 Biggest Mistakes Women Make in Dating and Love Relationships*, by Lyn Kelley, PhD:

When it comes to relationship commitment, we should think about it seriously and try to base our decision on rational thought. We have five guiding forces inside of us that assist us in making relationship decisions: our 'head' (brains, logic, intelligence), our 'gut' (intuition), our 'heart' (emotional, desire, passion), our 'chi' (life force, power, strength) and our 'vajayjay' (chemistry, sexual arousal). In regards to relationships, most people make mistakes when they lead with their 'heart' or 'vajayjay' and follow with their 'gut' and their 'head' and never even use their 'chi.'

The best way to make relationship choices is to lead with your 'head,' then use your 'gut,' then your 'chi,' then your 'heart,' and last, your 'vajayjay.' Write this down and read it over and over, every day. If men would use this method in the order I've described, they would make better choices as well.

Dr. Lyn Kelley, PhD is a Certified Professional Coach and to learn more about her go to www.janesgoodadvice.com.

Thank you for investing in yourselves to learn a little more about dating the "next" time around. It's definitely different than the first time around. Would you agree? Hopefully this has been informative for you and you'll have more success in the dating world (or at least a more positive with a better attitude!) So get on out there, you high-quality man/woman! Keep your chin up and enjoy the ride! In the end, it'll be worth it.

I'd love your feedback. My website is www.loveand-laughterlifcoaching.com. Reach out to me and give me your thoughts and opinions

Reflection Questions:
What mistakes am I willing to say I've made in my past, as it pertains to dating?

_____

_____

_____

_____

How can I be a more quality woman/man? What do I want my story to be when I meet my next spouse? (Whatever the decisions you're making now *will* be your story.)

_____

_____

_____

_____

If you picked three things you'll do differently in your dating life moving forward, what will those things be?

_____

_____

_____

_____

How will I support my single friends in their search?

_____
_____
_____
_____

What type of support do I need as I date?

_____
_____
_____
_____

What things will you specifically start praying about?

_____
_____
_____
_____

"The real purpose of life is just to be happy—to enjoy your life. To get to a place where you're not always trying to get someplace else. So many people spend their lives striving, trying to be someplace that they're not, they never get to arrive."
– Dr. Wayne Dyer

Bibliography

I'm not only including books in which I quote, but all the ones I've read these last few years. I'm sure with the reading of all these books, they've influenced my thinking without even knowing what book/CD/video/blog I obtained it. This will also be a great list of books for you to explore.

<u>Books</u>

Alsdorf, Debbie. *The Faith Dare*. Baker Publishing Group. 2010.

Behrendt, Greg and Amirra Routila-Begrendt. *It's Called a Break Up Because it's Broken. The Smart Girl's Break Up Buddy*. New York. Broadway books. 2005.

Behrendt, Greg and Amira Ruitola. *It's just a F***ing Date. Some Sort of Book About Dating*. New York. Diversionbooks 2013.

Brown, Bene. *The Gifts of Imperfection*. Center City, Minnesota. Hazelden. 2010.

Brown, Brene. *Daring Greatly*. New York. New York. Gotham Books. 2012.

Chapman, Gary. *The 5 Love Languages*. Chicago, IL. Northfield Publishing. 2011.

DeAngelis, Barbara. *Are You The One for Me? Knowing Who's Right and Avoiding Who's Wrong*. New York. Deli publishing.

Gottleib, Lori. *Marry Him...The Case for Settling for Mr. Good Enough*. London, England. New American Library 2010.

Gray, John. *Mars and Venus on a Date*. New York. Perennial Currents. 2005

Gunther, Randi, PhD Relationship Saboteurs. *Overcoming the Ten Behaviors That Undermine Love*. Oakland, CA. New Harbinger Publications, Inc. 2010.

Harvey, Steve. *Act Life a Lady, Think Like a Man*. New York, New York. Harper Collins Publications. 2014.

Hemmings, Jo. *Be Your Own Dating Coach*. Southern Gate Chipchester, West Sussex. England. Capstone. 2005.

Kirschner, Diana. *Love in 90 Days: The Essential Guide to Finding Your Own True Love*. New York. Center Street. 2009.

MacGraw, Dr. Phil. *Love Smart: Find the One You Want – Fix the One You Got*. New York. Free press. 2007

McCann, Jess. *You Lost Him at Hello. From Dating to "I Do" Secret Strategies from One of America's Top Dating Coaches*. Deerfield Beach, Florida. Health Communications, Inc. 2008.

McCann, Jess. *Was It Something I Said? The Answer to All Your Dating Dilemmas*. Guilford, Connecticut. Morris Publishing Group, LLC. 2013.

Page, Ken. *Deeper Dating: How to Drop the Games of Seduction and Discover the Power of Intimacy*. Boston. Shambhala. 2015.

Thomas, Gary. *The Sacred Search*. Colorado Springs, Colorado. Gary Thomas and associations with Yates and Yates. 2013. Print and DVD.

Thomas, Katherine Woodward. *Calling in "The One" 7 Weeks to Attract the Love of Your Life*. New York. Three Rivers Press. 2004.

Townsen, Dr John and Dr. Henry Cloud. *Boundaries in Dating*. Grand Rapids, Michigan. Zondervan. 2000. Print and DVD.

Walsh, Wendy Dr. *The 30 Day Love Detox*. New York. Rodale. 2013. Print and eBook.

eBooks

Fein, Ellen and Sherrie Schneider. *The Rules for Online Dating. Capturing the Heart of Mr. Right in Cyberspace*. New York. Pocket books. 2002. E-book.

Love, Midnite. (The Love Den Diaries- Mini-Series). *Think Like a Woman Always Be a Man*. Love Den Media Publishing. 2012. E-book.

Masters, Michael and Benjamin Burns. *Texting Appeal*. Masterdater Publishing. 2013. E-book.

McKay, Scot. *Deserve What You Want. Know Who You Are. What You Desire, and How to Get It*. Austin, TX. X and Y Communications. E-book.

Michaelson, Greg. *To Date a Man You Must Understand a Man: The Keys to Catch a Great Guy*. 2014. E-book.

Prager, Dennis. *Happiness is a Serious Problem*. Harper Collins e-books.

Torcivia, Phil. *The Nicest Guy and His Lonely Penis*. Smash Words. 2013. E-book.

Walker, Chris. *Xtreme Skills for Busy people. 22 Skills for Great Relation–ships*. E-book.

CD and DVD's

Carter, Christian. "Finding Love Online. Exactly What You Need to Know to Meet and Attract the Right Man Online." 2007. CD series.

"The Secret." TS production LLC. 2006. DVD.

Olsen, Jeff. "The Slight Edge. Turning Simple Disciplines into Massive Success." 2006 to 2008. Success books. 3 CD audiobook.

Stanley, Andy. "The New Rules for Love, Sex and Dating." Grand Rapids, MI. 2014. Zondervan. DVD series.

Other

The Steve Harvey Show. CBS.
https://www.youtube.com/watch?v=Ko2dDEnmI3s

Websites

BexBurton.DreamBuilderCoach.com

http://www.alternet.org/story/154699/the_absurd_myths_porn_teaches_us_about_sex

http://www.eharmony.com/dating-advice/#.VvBlvvkrI2w

http://www.eharmony.com/dating-advice/dating/steve-harvey-act-like-a-lady-think-like-a-man/#.VxUhoTArI2w

http://www.evanmarckatz.com/

http://www.fightthenewdrug.org/10-porn-stats-that-will-blow-your-mind/

http://innocentjustice.org/know-more/

https://www.iwf.org.uk/resources/trends

http://www.longdistancerelationships.net/faqs.htm

http://divorce.lovetoknow.com/Divorce_Statistics_and_Living_Together

http://madamenoire.com/135701/more-than-half-of-singles-have-sex-on-the-first-date/

https://www.match.com/y/article/index.aspx

http://www.match.com/magazine/article/5879/Online-Dating-Etiquette-Explained/#sthash.JQPNR9b1.dpuf

https://www.psychologytoday.com/blog/in-practice/201301/50-characteristics-healthy-relationships

http://www.toptenreviews.com/2-6-04.html

http://www.webroot.com/us/en/home/resources/tips/digital-family-life/internet-pornography-by-the-numbers http://www.webmd.com/sex/features/sex-dating-rules?page=2 https://www.youtube.com/watch?v=Ko2d-DEnmI3s

My Blog : https://lewisloveandlaughter.wordpress.com

Made in the USA
Charleston, SC
03 October 2016